A Career in Massage – Is it for you?

What massage schools and associations don't tell you about becoming a massage therapist…

Julie Onofrio, LMP

www.massage-career-guides.com

A Career in Massage – Is it for you?

ISBN 10: 0983977607

ISBN 13: 9780983977605

To Jack, Andrea, Cara and Supervision.

Acknowledgments

Thanks so much to Marina Ferguson for all her heartfelt editing and support. Thanks to Jack Blackburn for introducing me to the process of supervision and your continued support and cheering on. To my special supervision group for all the years of listening to me. Special thanks to Katherine for all that you do and have done through the many years.

Table of Contents

Introduction

I have been the sole proprietor of a massage business and a full time massage therapist since 1989. In 1987 I attended a 250-hour massage training program through Seattle Massage School (now Everest College). Through the many years of being a massage therapist, I have seen many people come and go and have been able to survive through the many challenges. The Associated Bodywork and Massage Professionals (one of the major professional associations, [ABMP]) collect statistics that show that approximately 60,000 new students join the massage profession each year while about 50,000 leave. (Patrick, "Massage Profession Metrics"). While we don't really know why they come and go, part of the problem could be that students are not well informed about the challenges ahead. I just know that they come in with energy and compassion and soon leave frustrated, broke and injured. Many hopefuls just jump into the profession without thoroughly investigating it. That was me too!

Although I have made a living for almost a quarter of a century in an unstable profession I can honestly say that it would have been a lot easier if there had been more training or information on how to get clients, how to keep them, how to keep from being injured, how to manage your money, how to manage your time, how to schedule, how to pay taxes, where to get insurance, how to keep burnout at bay; in short, the reality of being a massage therapist. Today, there are more resources and schools, but unfortunately there is also a great deal of hype and misinformation which makes the profession look different than it really is. Consequently, I decided to write this book to let you know the many challenges and the many possibilities available in this field.

People come to the massage profession for various reasons. Some come into the field after having been injured or faced with a health challenge that massage helped heal. Some come into massage looking for the freedom to schedule their own work life. Others only want part time work to supplement the family income. Many seek it as a second or even third career. Most massage therapists are female, single and average 44 years of age (Patrick, "Massage Profession Metrics"). Others respond to a 'calling' – a strong inner impulse to touch and help others. All of the above are valid reasons for pursuing a massage therapy career but these reasons are the exact factors that can also lead to burnout, career ending injuries, and inadequate cash flow, making a career in massage difficult. Despite all of these less-than-favorable statistics and facts, a career in massage can be a financially, emotionally and spiritually rewarding career when you enter the career path as a more informed participant...and that is what you are about to do.

Sit down with your favorite cup of tea or coffee and get ready to explore the truth about becoming a massage therapist and hopefully find inspiration to continue on your path -whatever that may be! You are about to discover how you can make a difference in people's lives while making a great living.

To Your Success,

Julie Onofrio, LMP

(Licensed Massage Practitioner)

Seattle, WA

Chapter 1. The Wonderful World of Careers in Massage

Massage Therapy Careers are often talked about as one of the up-and-coming careers. U.S. News & World Report (Grant, "The 50 Best Careers of 2011") lists Careers in Massage in their top 50 careers for 2011. The Bureau of U.S. Labor and Statistics ("Occupational Outlook Handbook") says that the massage field has a faster than average growth rate and expects a "19 percent increase from 2008 to 2018". The latest survey from the American Massage Therapy Association cites that in 2010, massage therapy was a $12-17 billion industry, which is a significant increase from their estimate in 2005, when they said massage therapy was only a $6 to $11 billion a year industry.

There are now many massage franchises that provide new jobs by offering low-cost massage through membership programs. Spas are the biggest employers of massage therapists. Day spas, destination resorts and cruise ships provide relaxation and relief from stress. Medical spas provide therapeutic massage. Massage therapy is being accepted more in many states as part of health care and more insurance companies are just starting to pay for massage services when an injury or condition can be helped by massage. Research, which provides evidence of the effectiveness of massage, is being done by the Massage Therapy Foundation and the Touch Research Institute and many others. Massage has been shown to be helpful for carpal tunnel syndrome, back pain, neck pain, foot pain, anxiety, depression, fibromyalgia and many other health conditions.

From birth to death, massage can help ease the passage through life. Premature infants have been shown to thrive with structured touch. Massage augments the relaxing, getaway experience and is routinely used at vacation resorts. Medical spas and massage clinics provide massage for sports injuries, work injuries and car accidents as well as many medical conditions such as fibromyalgia and numerous other pain syndromes. Massage is also finding its way into hospitals for recovery from surgery and illness. Professional athletes are using massage to enhance their performance as well as to help prevent injuries. Massage helps women through pregnancy and childbirth and through hormonal changes such as premenstrual syndrome and menopause. It can help ease the discomfort of the end stage of life in hospices, nursing homes and assisted living centers. Each year, as the figures show, bring more and more people to massage.

According to the Bureau of Labor and Statistics ("Occupational Employment Statistics") annual wages for a massage therapist range from $17k to $68K. Many massage schools claim that you can make $60 or more an hour and that you can work when you want and for as long as you want. Some massage schools have teamed up with massage franchises to provide jobs for massage students right out of massage school. There are countless job opportunities at spas and resorts, on cruise ships and for chiropractors and doctors.

Most people choose a career in massage because they want a job or business in which they feel they make a difference. They want a career that is more meaningful. They may be tired of the 9-5 job stress and struggles. They might have been told that they have good hands and are good at massaging spouses, friends and family members. Some come to the profession because they have been helped by massage for an injury or chronic condition or they have experienced one of the many other benefits of massage and want to provide the same for others. Finally, some come to massage as a way of being of service to others. Many massage therapists say it isn't about the money but it is about helping others.

In 1987 when I went to massage school the only jobs in massage were the independent contractor positions which really meant you were self employed. Incidentally, I was fortunate to start in

Seattle where massage was more accepted than in some other parts of the country. In 1989, in western New York State, where I am from, massage therapy was considered to be a shady business and some neighborhoods did not welcome a massage therapist. Today, all that has changed as more and more massage franchises and massage businesses open their doors providing massage to local communities. While there are more jobs available than ever, most massage therapists eventually start their own business at some time in their career.

The many advertisements that entice vacationers to resorts or spas show luxury massage suites. Massage schools also advertise the end product with pictures of smiling therapists and glowing candles. You can almost hear the soft music playing and smell the lavender. Everyone is so relaxed and happy and beautiful! Life couldn't be better when you are getting a massage or giving a massage! Everyone is healthy and fit and happy in a career in massage! Or are they?

Chapter 2.
The Truth about Careers in Massage

There are three main areas of interest that you need to know about when you are considering a career in massage – the salary statistics (how much can you make?), job opportunities (where can you work and find higher paying jobs?) and the fact that most massage therapists start their own business (how and why?). I'll list these areas and then tell you the truth so you can make a more informed decision and decide if a career in massage is right for you.

Salaries

How much can you really make as a massage therapist? The problem with salary statistics from various massage associations and the Bureau of Labor and Statistics is that they vary greatly. Many therapists only work part time and most are self-employed. Job statistics, unfortunately, will not include this vital information. The latest report from the American Massage Therapy Association (AMTA) says:

> "In 2010, the average annual income for a massage therapist (including tips) who provides approximately 15 hours of massage per week was estimated to be $31,980, compared to $37,123 for 2009. The reduction in income reflects both a decrease in the number of average hours worked and lower numbers for consumer use of massage in 2010."

The Associated Bodywork and Massage Professionals (ABMP) reports:

> "Average massage-related income for massage therapists in 2007 was $17,750, with a median income of $15,500 (2007 ABMP Member Survey)."

Those figures are up from 2005 where they reported that the average massage-related income for massage therapists in 2005 was $18,950, with a median income of $14,500 (2005 ABMP Member Survey).

Also from the ABMP website www.massagetherapy.com:

- "Total earnings by massage therapists, <u>including their earnings from other employment</u>, averaged $34,141 (2007 ABMP Member Survey)."

- "First-year practice average income was $10,503, reflecting the challenges of establishing a professional-service practice (2007 ABMP Member Survey)."

The Bureau of Labor Statistics ("Occupational Employment Statistics") says:

"Median *hourly* wages of massage therapists, including gratuities, were $16.78 in May 2008. The middle 50 percent earned between $11.36 and $25.14. The lowest 10 percent earned less than $8.01, and the highest 10 percent earned more than $33.47. Because many therapists work part time, yearly earnings can vary considerably, depending on the therapist's schedule. Generally, massage therapists earn some portion of their income as gratuities."

Massage schools often say that you can make $60 an hour or more working as a massage therapist. They also say that you will have the freedom to work the hours that you would like and come and go as you please.

The Truth: Sixty dollars an hour is the average amount that is charged <u>to the client</u> for a massage in the US. That is the fee that is paid for a massage. This sounds like a great salary for a massage therapist but the truth is that you really don't make that amount. If you work for someone else as a subcontractor, you will only be paid 20-40% of that amount or you will be paid a flat hourly rate. That means you will be paid $12-$25 per hour for hands-on massage work. In addition, when you don't have a client you will be paid even less or may not be paid at all for that time. You will probably be doing other tasks such as cleaning or paperwork. Entry level positions at the many massage franchises start at $12 an hour and again, you only get paid that when you are giving a massage. Your income will often depend on tips which vary with services rendered and the current economy.

Full time work in the massage profession is usually 20-25 hours per week and often less because of the physical demands of the work. When you do the math, working 25 hours at $12 an hour will hardly pay the bills after taxes. You may be able to set your own hours, but at that rate of pay it is difficult to make a living. In order to really come and go as you please, as in any other job or career, requires having an income that supports that lifestyle.

Most massage therapists go on to start their own business at some point in their career because they can usually make more money per hour. Unfortunately, it still won't be the $60+ an hour that is promised by some massage schools. Realistically, when you set up your own business, you will have to deduct expenses like office rent, phone, laundry and advertising. You will be paying your own taxes, health insurance and vacation pay. You will have to learn how to promote your business and get clients on your massage table. You can usually make more money if you are business savvy and can keep your expenses low and your income high. You can set your own hours, but being in business requires that you show up when clients want a massage which may not always be as convenient as it seems. You can set your own office hours, but you will need to work enough hours to make ends meet.

What you make is also determined by the number of hours that you can physically, emotionally and mentally do massage. Giving a massage is a physically demanding process. It requires good health and stamina. Giving massage can be emotionally stressful because of dealing with people who are in pain or in distress. Subsequently, since massage is physically and emotionally demanding, most massage therapists rarely work more than 25-30 hours a week. For massage therapists, that number of hours is considered full time. If you try to work more hours a week, the risk of injury and burnout increases. Your income is also limited by the fact that you can only see one client at a time. There are only so many hours in a day. So, no matter what path you choose – a job or starting your own business, it will require that you work enough hours to make a living.

The key to success is making more per hour while working the least number of hours. You can learn specialized massage techniques or work with specific populations to add more value to your services so that you can charge more for your services. There are many other ways to supplement your income or increase your income. Teaching massage classes to groups such as couples, families, mothers/infants, schools and church groups can help increase your earnings as well as help you build your massage business. You can also sell products such as massage oils and lotions or aromatherapy supplies. I have used my experience of being a massage therapist for almost 24 years to create websites about massage for massage therapists and for the general public to bring in additional income. I also have extensive training in Structural Integration and Trigger point therapy, allowing me to charge higher-than-usual rates. Other options down the line are to set up a clinic, spa or other facility and hire massage therapists to do the work or buy a massage franchise. You can also become a teacher of massage at a massage school or teach your own continuing education classes to supplement your income.

Despite the bleak statistics, you can make a good living as a massage therapist if you have the courage to find or create higher paying jobs for yourself or create a massage business that is financially lucrative. That is accomplished by learning everything you can about how to run a business, learning effective marketing and by maintaining boundaries in your practice. Finding or creating a higher paying job is really more about your job-finding skills than the actual massage skills, but you will need to be able to do a good massage too!

Jobs in Massage Therapy

Jobs in massage therapy are often made to sound very appealing by the high rate of pay that was just shown to be inaccurate. Pictures of therapists working in a relaxing spa with people who are in good physical shape, all with smiling faces, are shown on many brochures and websites of massage employers. As massage has become more in demand, more jobs for therapists are becoming available.

The Truth: Massage is a great new business opportunity but unfortunately, many shop owners are not massage therapists so they don't really understand what therapists need. Many massage employers frequently take massage therapists for granted. Employers may impose low pay, long hours, no breaks, and no vacation or sick pay or health insurance. I personally have seen therapists work under very stressful conditions, especially for chiropractors and franchises or other situations where the end goal is often more about money than service. Those massage therapists ended up with injuries or career-ending problems in addition to financial challenges. Working for a low pay may create resentment that can impact your work. A low pay may preclude you from getting a regular weekly massage (which is essential in this profession) because you won't be able to afford it. Long hours without breaks can take a toll on the body and energy. Being on your feet all day and using your hands and arms repetitively set you up for an increased risk for carpal tunnel syndrome, tendonitis and other injuries. All of these can be career-ending conditions.

As an employee you will also be faced with other challenges such as working on people that you don't feel comfortable with. For example, you may be asked to work on pregnant women or people recovering from cancer, even though you may have not had adequate training in these areas. As an employee you are required to listen to the boss or risk losing your job. Many massage employers are not massage therapists themselves and often do not understand the risk of doing massage under certain conditions. You may also be asked to work with people who have less than ideal hygiene or are beyond your strength or other capabilities. You may not be able to have much say in the matter when you are an employee.

Many spas and clinics will also require that you sell their memberships or retail products in addition to giving massages. They may give you financial incentives for doing so, but you will need to acquire sales skills. Many massage therapists think that having a job will allow them to get out of 'selling to clients'. Selling seems to be a scary word for many massage therapists because all they really want to do is give a great massage.

Your income as a massage employee will also include and be dependent on getting tips from clients. Because of the many economic challenges in recent years, tips are often the first thing to be eliminated from people's spending. There is also some controversy over whether tips are appropriate for massage therapists as they are becoming a part of the health care profession. Employers may often give you salary quotes that include tips.

As an employee, you may be asked to sign a non-compete clause, which will limit your ability to work after you leave the job. A non-compete clause means you may not be able to take clients with you when you leave, or work within a certain area. This can severely limit your career opportunities in the future.

However grim these facts seem it is possible to find a good job with an employer who respects you and pays you what you deserve to make. You just have to keep looking until you find such a place. They do exist!

Your Own Massage Business

Most massage schools offer some training in how to start and run a business. It is usually a very short part of the curriculum and gives you an over-view of what you will need to do. Starting your own business will allow you to make much more per hour and give you more freedom but will also require that you have the skills to fill your schedule with clients.

The Truth: Most massage schools offer a very basic class in how to start and run a business but it is really not enough. To be successful you need a degree or background in business, marketing and customer service or you must be willing to learn. Having your own business means that you will have to know how to start it and keep it going. You will have to know about marketing, bookkeeping, insurance billing, customer service and much more. Here are the important things you will have to do:

- Get a business license or whatever is required for your city/state/county
- Create a business and marketing plan
- Set up a business bank account

- Set up an accounting system to keep track of income and expenses
- Find a location, rent an office and sign a lease or contract
- Set up an office with massage table, reception area, phone/fax/computer
- Provide water and a safe environment
- Learn to bill insurance, track billing and payments, bill for co-pays or even appear in court
- Set up a website to get new clients and allow clients to purchase gift certificates and make online appointments
- Set up and use Facebook and Twitter to market yourself
- Join the chamber of commerce or other business networking groups
- Learn to network with doctors, physical therapists, chiropractors and other health care professionals
- Give presentations at health fairs
- Give free massage at community events or sports events

- Do laundry or pay a laundry service
- Deal directly with clients on issues like no shows, late arrivals or last minute cancellations
- Take continuing education classes

Being successful in a massage business has little to do with any special technique or general knowledge of massage. It has more to do with who you are - your beliefs about money and success, your ability to learn and your commitment to making a business successful. However, there are many resources in the form of books, online courses, business and massage associations that will help you learn how to build a successful practice.

If you choose to be self-employed as a sole proprietor, be aware that you will do all of the work. You will be the technician, business planner, marketing manager, office manager, receptionist, bookkeeper, janitor and customer service department. Michael Gerber talks about this in his book *The Emyth Revisited*, saying that small businesses are started by people who are 'technicians' and have something that they love doing but don't have a clue how to make it into a business. As a massage business owner you will need to learn to be a business person. You will be the one that establishes boundaries and policies to support your business such as your fee for services, last-minute no shows or cancellations and dealing with other difficulties with clients. And last but not least you will have to learn to separate yourself from your business. As Gerber says in his book,

"Your business is not your life".

As a group, massage therapists struggle with this issue all the time because 'How can you charge for something so wonderful as a massage?' 'How can you charge for caring?' What needs to be understood is that although what you do is a personal experience for both you and the client, it is still a business. To continue successfully in the business you must be paid. Your skills are very valuable and you deserve to be paid for your time. The caring is free! By remembering that you are running a business you can continue in a meaningful career that makes you the money that you need to live and support yourself.

So whether you choose to follow the path of employment or starting your own business, you can be successful and make a living as a massage therapist.

Chapter 3.
Who Needs Massage?

The Demand for Massage Therapists

How big is the demand for massage therapists? We really don't know because the statistics are contradictory, but the evidence supports the trend of a growing field. More people are getting massage regularly and more are using it to combat stress, injuries and various diseases and conditions.

According to the American Massage Therapy Association's (AMTA) Massage Therapy Industry Fact Sheet: "In 2005, massage therapy was projected to be a $6 to $11 billion a year industry". AMTA estimates that in 2010, massage therapy was a $12-17 billion industry.

The Associated Bodywork and Massage Professionals (ABMP) reports in their media section that

"Consumers receive approximately 230 million massage sessions annually, making massage therapy an $11 billion to $15 billion industry" ("Massage Therapy Fast Facts").

According to the 2010 AMTA consumer survey, an average of 18% of adult Americans received at least one massage between July 2009 and July 2010, and an average of 28% of adult Americans received a massage in the previous five years. That leaves 82% of the population for therapists to educate and market massage.

ABMP: In 2009, 86% of respondents did not see a massage therapist. Fully 19% of them said they simply didn't perceive a value or feel a massage was necessary. Thirty-nine percent cited cost as a deterrent, but with 90% of massage sessions paid out of pocket, a prevailing cost of $1 per minute is outside the means of some budgets.

The Truth: While it is nice to know how much of a demand there is for massage therapy, the demand for massage therapists has little to do with your ability to be successful. The demand for massage varies greatly in different states, cities and towns because there is a wide variation in acceptance of massage nationwide. There is still much work to be done in getting public acceptance and educating the public as to the therapeutic benefits of massage. Unfortunately, massage is often used as a front for prostitution and human trafficking. Although massage has been around for many years as a healing modality, it is still in its infancy and way behind other professions such as physical therapy as a recognized modality of healing.

Massage is also **not** widely accepted by insurance companies or the medical profession at this time. In most states you can bill car insurance companies for massage therapy for car accidents or worker's compensation for work-related injuries. Major medical still does not cover relaxation or therapeutic massage except in Washington State and Florida. Here in Washington, we are contracted providers with insurance companies, but each year the pay rate and maximum number of sessions allowed are reduced, making it harder to make a living through insurance work. More insurance companies in other states are starting to "pay willingly" for massage but it is difficult to find out who is paying and who is not.

Massage has and is being used to treat many health conditions such as muscle pain and dysfunction along with headaches, fibromyalgia and stress. Scientific research is beginning to provide evidence of the benefits of massage.

The Demand for Men in the Massage Profession

Many massage schools also ignore the challenges that men will have in the massage profession. Men are the minority in this field. Eighty-five percent of all massage therapists in the U.S. are women. Women often prefer getting a massage from a woman for safety issues and men also seem to have issues with getting a massage from a male. People with previous abuse issues by men may find getting a massage from a man uncomfortable. Part of the problem is self perpetuated by the massage profession itself. Spas and other employers will ask people who are calling for an appointment whether or not they prefer a female or male as if they should be concerned about the issue. The bottom line is if you are a male and you think you will have problems – you most likely will. The way to get through this issue is to market yourself in a way that addresses these issues and help people overcome their past issues of abuse and trust. Getting a regular massage from a male may actually work to heal these issues. Another way is to focus on more medically oriented massage and work in the health care profession rather than in the relaxation and spa areas.

See also:
Bayer, Cary. "You Are in High Demand." Massage Today.
<http://www.massagetoday.com/mpacms/mt/article.php?id=13194>.

Chute, Robert. "Man Power Male Therapists Talk About Discrimination."
<http://www.massagetherapy.com/articles/index.php/article_id/1381/Man-Power>.

Osborn, Karrie. "Gender in the Profession: Massage from Mars or Venus?" <http://www.massagetherapy.com/articles/index. php/article_id/1376/Gender-in-the-Profession>.

Chapter 4.
What Type of Massage Should You Study?

The field of massage and bodywork is constantly growing. Massage is often referred to as bodywork. What exactly is massage and what is bodywork? The two terms are often confusing because, even professionally, the terms massage and bodywork have not been clearly defined. Some think that 'bodywork' is a type of massage while others think that 'massage' is a type of bodywork. There are still others who think that the term 'bodywork' should be kept in the auto industry. Massage is often thought of as basic Swedish massage. Bodywork is usually a word used by massage therapists who have more training in various techniques and their work with clients involves a specific goal.

Most schools start by teaching basic Swedish massage. For some reason this has become the norm. One of the little-known things about licensing is that some states will exclude some therapies such as Reiki, Reflexology and/or Structural Integration from the licensing requirements. Check with the State Board of Massage in the state where you will work to find out what exclusions there are, if any. You may still have to get training and certification in one of those types of therapies in order to practice but you may not have to learn basic Swedish massage or go to a formal massage school. For instance: in WA State, you are able to practice reflexology (a type of foot zone massage) without going to massage school and getting a massage license.

ABMP reports that there are over 250 different types of massage and bodywork modalities available. New forms of massage or bodywork are being developed daily. People are drawn to various types of massage for various reasons. Since each person has different needs for touch and touch is perceived on an individual basis, the potential in the massage field is unlimited. Swedish massage is a good place to start as it is simple to learn and it is a good way to become comfortable with touching people. As a massage therapist you will be constantly learning new things and taking various classes in different types of massage. It is one of the great attractions in the massage field because you will be constantly learning.

Medical massage is one of the latest courses of study being offered at many massage schools. There is still much confusion over what medical massage is. There is not one specific technique called medical massage as some may lead you to believe. Any type of massage can be called medical massage if knowledge of pathology and how massage helps that pathology is used to create an outcome-based session. Any type of massage can be used including Swedish massage. Medical massage does not require that you have any specific training or experience. There are some people and massage schools that are offering something called **"Medical Massage"** which makes it confusing. It isn't a specific technique or method but rather a way of assessing a client's physical condition and creating a plan to work with the person and his or her condition. Even more confusing is that there is also something called *Medical Massage* that comes out of the old Soviet Union that is being taught by a few of their descendants. *Russian Medical Massage* is a specific technique but it is not the only way to do medical massage. Just be sure to ask more questions if your school is telling you that you will be learning medical massage. What do they mean by that exactly?

You will have several types of massage that you can choose from in your massage school program after learning basic Swedish massage. Some of the most popular are deep tissue massage, sports massage, pregnancy massage, hot stone massage and reflexology. The best way to decide a course of study is to first read about some of the many different types of massage and what they do. You can read more on my website www.massage-career-guides.com in the section on different types of massage. Then if any call to you, go and find a massage therapist that does that type of work and get a few sessions. Talk to the massage therapist and ask about how and why they use that type of massage. See if getting that type of massage makes a difference to how you feel.

The nice thing about having so many different types of massage is that you can study them at any time and most therapists study many different techniques throughout their career. Continuing education classes are required in many states to renew your massage license so you will be continually learning new methods. Most types of massage require that you study and practice a method for a few years before you can actually claim you are providing that service, although many will call themselves specialists in areas like deep tissue massage and pregnancy massage after a weekend workshop. Becoming an expert and practicing a form of massage for a year or two can be a big help in your marketing efforts for your business or give you an added boost when looking for a job.

Chapter 5. Licensing, Legislation and Certification

In order to practice massage professionally you need to know what licensing and/or certification requirements are required by your state, city, town and/or county. You will need to understand the laws about practicing massage and your allowed scope of practice (what you can and can't do as a massage therapist).

Licensing is different from certification. Certification is a voluntary process that is set up by individual types of therapies and massage schools. When you graduate from a massage school, you will get a certificate of completion that will allow you to apply for a license from your state if required – you are certified by the massage school. Each state regulates the practice of massage through various massage or health care boards and creates rules and regulations around the massage licensing process. Each state has a different massage licensing requirement but there are six states that don't have any requirements at this time. To get a license to practice massage you will have to complete various educational and testing requirements along with other things such as fingerprinting or background checks as outlined in each state's regulations. Sometimes even though the state offers professional licensing, individual cities will require other permits such as a massage establishment permit. Most unregulated states **do** regulate massage on a local level. Visit www.municode.com and click on "online codes" to search for local regulations.

Most states that require licensing use a test created by the National Certification Board for Therapeutic Massage and Bodywork (NCBTMB) or a test called the Massage & Bodywork Licensing Examination (MBLEx) created by the Federation of Massage Therapy Boards (FSMTB). The NCBTMB actually offers two different exams – The National

Certification Examination for Therapeutic Massage and Bodywork (NCETMB) and the National Certification Examination for Therapeutic Massage (NCETM). The eligibility requirements are the same for the two exams. What is different is the focus of the questions. The NCETMB includes questions about bodywork assessment and application. There are also a few states such as Oregon that have their own method of testing and do not accept either of these two exams and require a massage practical (hands on) exam.

The term National Certification Exam (NCE) that is used to describe the two exams administered by the National Certification Board for Therapeutic Massage and Bodywork (NCBTMB) is misleading. Taking the NCE does not mean you are actually *nationally* certified and can practice in any state that accepts this exam. Each state that requires or uses the exam as a part of their licensing requirements also has different educational requirements that must also be met. The actual certification part may also be voluntary – meaning you can take the exam that is required by your state but you have to pay extra fees to the NCBTMB to actually be nationally certified by them. Even if you pay the extra fees to become nationally certified, it does not mean that you can practice in any state. You will still need a license in whatever state you work in and you will need to fulfill their requirements for massage licensing. There is also an advanced credentialing exam that is in the planning stages that will be voluntary.

In the past few years the NCBTMB has been under scrutiny by the massage profession. Many top executives and board members have resigned over the internal struggles. Most recently the American Massage Therapy Association who was instrumental in creating the NCBTMB has accepted the exam from the Federation of Massage Therapy Board and rejected their support of the NCBTMB. This was a very big statement by the NCBTMB founders. Currently the NCBTMB is working on these issues and is aware of the problems. The Alliance for Massage Therapy Education has recently asked the NCBTMB to stop offering their exam and focus on the advanced certification program which is creating stress

in the massage profession. (http://www.afmte.org/2011/05/05/alliance-offers-new-vision-for-national-certification/). Welcome to the world of massage politics.

It will be up to you to find out the licensing and education requirements of your state. The most up-to-date listings will be on your state massage board's website. Look for the number of hours of education required in each category, along with any requirements that a school be accredited or approved of by the state. Some states will have a list of approved schools that you can choose from.

Some massage schools are also accredited which is a voluntary process that the schools choose to go through (unless it is required by their state). Accreditation is a process that makes the massage school take a look at how they teach and reach students. The main reason for being an accredited school is also to get more federal grant and loan assistance for students. Accreditation, however, is not an absolute mark of a program's quality. There are many exceptional programs that are not accredited and also accredited institutions that are substandard.

According to ABMP reports:

> Only 29 percent of the approximately 1,500-plus state-approved massage schools are accredited by one or more of the six bodies approved by the U.S. Department of Education to accredit massage programs. Accordingly, we believe the three states that only license graduates of accredited massage schools are misguided. ("Public Policy and Licensing")

Schools can be accredited separately from programs. In other words, an accredited school can offer a massage program that is not accredited. One of the accreditation agencies that you will hear about most often is the Commission of Massage Therapy Accreditation (COMTA). This agency accredits about 300 of the 1500+ massage schools that are out there. COMTA was started by the AMTA but is now a separate agency. There are also about 6 other accrediting agencies for the massage profession.

Again, the massage schools that you will be researching should also have this information but it is good to have it before hand to make sure the school you choose will meet the requirements. You can also check with the state board to find out if there are any problems with the school or if they are being investigated for any problems.

Currently, there are three states that require massage schools to be accredited. The number may change when you go to massage school. Be wary if you are required to go to an accredited school and that the school you are thinking of attending claims they are in the process of getting accredited. The school must be accredited by the time you graduate or it may not count. There is a whole chapter on choosing a massage school to help you research and decide if a career in massage is for you.

See also: Korn, Cliff . "An Accreditation Quagmire." <u>Massage Today</u>.
<http://www.massagetoday.com/mpacms/mt/article.php?id=12063>.

Chapter 6.
Touching Others/Helping Others

Being a massage therapist means that you will make your living touching others with their clothes half off or really mostly off (but covered with sheets or blankets of some sort). While this may seem obvious to many, it somehow gets overlooked and people enter massage school not knowing that touching people may be an issue for some. It also means that you will be getting massages yourself in massage school and dealing with personal modesty and touch issues. Spouses and family members may also find this uncomfortable.

Touch has a way of bringing up emotional, mental and spiritual issues and will definitely influence the massage sessions you do. Our bodies hold our innermost feelings and memories. When you work with clients you will need to be aware that massage may bring up emotional responses in people at any time. Post-traumatic stress disorders or previous trauma can cause such a reaction. Grief and sadness is another thing that is held deeply in the body. People may cry, yell, laugh and even jump off your table in fear during treatment. Just the slightest touch can sometimes create a very strong emotional response. You will need to be able to handle whatever comes up, which means dealing with your own issues as well. So even though the act of doing massage is mainly physical, people are more than just a body lying on the table.

Touch is one of the first ways infants learn about themselves; where they end and another begins. The early attachment to parents or caregivers is the basis for building healthy self-esteem and self-confidence. The early experiences of touch influence a person's life in ways that we don't yet thoroughly understand. When giving a massage, clients do not care about what technique you are doing – whether you doing effleurage or pettrissage (two types of basic massage strokes). What they do know is how it feels to them. They may feel cared for, held, valued and nurtured. You can do the exact same thing on each person and each person will feel something different. One may feel relief and one may feel more pain or stress. Nurturing touch to one person may feel like a violation to others.

Another issue that often develops for men receiving massage is an erection. Since you will be touching people and that includes men, there is a good chance that an erection will occur. It is just a natural physiological response to touch. You will learn in massage school how to handle this. The real problem lies with men thinking that the massage you are giving will have a "happy ending". Massage is often used to advertise and cover up prostitution. This creates problems in the massage profession because people may be confused when going for a legitimate massage. Touch is sensual in nature, as in "of the senses," but there is a big difference between sensual and sexual in our world today. Unfortunately, there are many illegal massage parlors advertising massage services when in fact they are offering something else.

There will be a time when you will get that call looking for that 'something else'. The caller may say things like "Do you do full body massage?" emphasizing the "full". People may also contact you asking 'what you look like' or to 'send them a picture of yourself'. Both are totally inappropriate. However, the fact is that men do get erections on the massage table and even the most respectful of men can have moments of weakness and ask for that "happy ending". I have also heard stories of men being approached by women for sexual favors in a massage so it can happen both ways. Your safety is first. You will learn to set boundaries to keep yourself safe in these situations and learn to separate the natural erections from those wanting more. Just know that you will have to deal with it at some time in your career.

Helping Others – On Being a Helper

So many massage therapists come to the massage profession thinking that they just want to help others and have a more meaningful career. While wanting to help is what often brings people to a career in massage, it can also be what makes it difficult to survive in the field. Massage therapists work with people who need help in solving some problem such as pain, stress or other health conditions. Because people seek out massage therapists for help, it creates the dynamics of a helping relationship, which implies that there is one person who knows more. This creates a power differential in the relationship between the massage therapist and the client. The client will look up to the massage therapist and hope for help when often the answer is really within the client. A good massage therapist will be able to assist a client in becoming aware of their own answers. It is done more through listening than actually doing or saying anything.

While this may seem unimportant, there really is much more to helping than meets the eye. Often helping is a way to get your unmet needs taken care of which will make the massage session more about you than the client. The massage session should always have the client in mind first at all times otherwise the client is deprived of the care they deserve and are paying for. Underneath the need to help is often an unconscious unmet need. Because it is an unconscious process, it is difficult to understand and deal with. This power differential sets the roles of the massage therapist and client. The client will often act towards the therapist in ways that remind him or her of a former authority such as their parents or significant people from their early childhood years. To put it really simply – the client will act like the child and think that the massage therapist is a parent figure. This is called transference. The client is trying to get their early needs met from the massage therapist or will act out their old patterns. It doesn't happen all the time, but it will happen. It is a part of everyday relationships too. It isn't a bad thing and it may be one way that people can heal the past.

The best way to deal with transference is to not play into other people's projections and maintain your professional boundaries. Boundaries are not only the physical boundaries but the policies and procedures that support your role as a massage therapist. Boundaries include simple things like setting fees, setting hours and setting cancellation policies. They include rules for dating clients and being friends with clients or being in dual relationships with clients. Dual relationships are when your client is also your dentist or accountant and you have different roles at different times. It can create a challenge when it comes to maintaining boundaries and being able to focus on them only as a client when you are doing massage. Becoming more aware of yourself by creating and maintaining boundaries will help you grow as a massage therapist and will assist you in serving your clients.

The flip side of this issue is countertransference, which is the way the massage therapist tries to get their needs met through the client relationship. This often leads to less-than-desirable situations and can also directly influence the success of the massage therapist. Again, it is often an unconscious process, especially in the beginning. Even now as you are thinking about a massage career, your idea of helping others may just seem like part of the natural process. You may think you are helping because it is the right thing to do, but often there is another side to helping such as getting appreciation, acceptance and recognition.

The need to help and give advice is seen as countertransference and may lead to burnout in the massage profession. Helping others without taking care of yourself first can leave you feeling drained, injured or without adequate financial support to stay in business or pay your bills. When a massage therapist does things like gives up their lunch hour to work on clients or change their schedule to accommodate clients it can eventually lead to feeling resentful. Massage therapists also often feel a need to offer low-cost massage thinking it is a way to get new clients and keep them coming back. Charging less than you need to make is really a boundary issue. When you charge less and sacrifice your income for the chance of getting a client, it can increase your chance of ending up in burnout.

There will be many challenges throughout your career that will require you to take a look at yourself and keep the therapeutic relationship clear with the client. You will learn more about this in a good massage school but again, some schools do not cover it. As you start working with more clients in your career, the process of supervision can help you to create your ideal practice and provide support for you throughout your career. This is the process of periodically talking about your challenges with a more experienced massage therapist. (There is a chapter on it later.) It is a fairly new concept and not always offered in massage school. Understanding the underlying reasons why you are in this profession will help you be more successful. The more self aware you become, the easier it will be for you to create boundaries to support yourself in the process of becoming a massage therapist. The solution to helping is a good self-care program. I have a separate chapter on self care later in this book.

Chapter 7.
Choosing a Massage School

The process of looking into massage schools can also help you make your decision to become a massage therapist. You can learn a lot about the massage profession from researching massage schools.

Choosing to go to massage school can be a major life-altering experience no matter what phase or situation you are currently in. It will require that you change your daily schedule to include classes, studying, reading and doing the required practice massages. You will also be learning new things that may have you step outside of your comfort zone. You will not only learn about anatomy and physiology, you will learn to touch people in mean-ingful and healing ways. This requires that you look at your own issues around touch and also be learning more about yourself through touch and by giving massages and getting massage. The way to choose a massage school is to know what you need and find a massage school that matches those needs. Various employers will also prefer graduates from certain schools so you can start to investigate places to work before you go to massage school asking them for this information if you plan on getting a job when you graduate.

Researching and choosing a massage school is important because different schools will focus on different areas. There are schools that are more technically oriented, focusing on the physical anatomy and how massage affects the body and there are schools that focus more on the body-mind connection. There are also many different combinations of those two types. It is also important to keep in mind that massage schools are businesses that are seeking students to keep them in business. A good massage school should be concerned about the quality of therapists that they turn out and will be open to many of the issues discussed in this book.

There are over 1,500 massage schools in the United States ("The Phenomenal Growth in Number of Massage Schools"). There is a wide variety of what schools teach, the number of hours in which they teach and the way they teach. Each state requires that classes meet certain requirements and therefore are regulated by the state massage board. You must inform yourself about the number of hours of training required in each course for your state or the state you want to work in. Unfortunately, each state has different requirements and massage licenses are not easily transferable to other states. You will also need to know if your state requires that you go to an approved or accredited school. You should know what testing is required to obtain a professional massage license in your state. You can find this information by going to your state massage board's website and contacting them for the specific information.

With so many massage schools to choose from, the process of researching massage schools can be overwhelming. You can find out massage licensing requirements and find lists of massage schools on my website at www.massage-career-guides.com.

But remember, massage schools like any other profession, don't really teach you how to be a massage therapist. What they teach is how to massage. Being able to apply what you learned in school, find a job or build a business after massage school depends more on you and your commitment and love for massage. Massage schools will do the best to set you on your way but it is really a much bigger task than a 500-1,000 hour massage school program can realistically produce.

As with anything else there are good and bad massage schools. What is good for one person may not be good for another. The key to choosing a massage school is to find one that fits your needs and learning style. What you get out of massage school also depends on what you put into it. The bonus is that you will definitely learn about yourself.

Massage schools come in many sizes with a wide variety of curriculums. Community colleges and technical colleges are now offering massage programs at a lower rate. There are also many small 'mom and pop' or independently owned massage schools whose owners have been in the business for years. Some are owned by massage therapists or other health-care practitioners. Recently there has been a surge of large massage school chains such as Cortiva and Corinthian College buying the smaller, individually owned massage schools. There are advantages and disadvantages to both. Smaller schools offer smaller class sizes and more individual attention. Smaller schools may be harder hit by the economy. The larger schools may offer a larger network when it comes time to finding a job or starting your business. Both may be hiring less-than-adequate teachers because of the lack of qualified teachers that has resulted from the phenomenal growth of massage schools in the last 20 years.

The state massage board may or, more often may not, regulate massage schools. Schools will sometimes go through an accreditation process with an individual accrediting agency. It is difficult to compare schools and to decide what training you will need to be a successful massage therapist as there are no set curriculums or standards in massage school. The type of classes and number of hours of training vary from school to school.

There are many things to take into consideration when choosing a massage school that have more to do with your needs but also will fulfill the requirements for you to legally practice massage in your state/city:

- What type of learner are you and what style of teaching does a school offer?
- The location-- is it close and convenient?
- Class schedule -- are there evening or day-time hours and weekend classes-- hours that fit your schedule or can be made to fit?
- Number of hours of training-- does it fill the licensing requirement and your needs?
- Cost of classes-- is it within your budget?

- Policies and procedures of schools-- what will you be responsible for and what will the school provide?

- Teacher's abilities and credentials-- are the teachers actually trained as teachers or just massage therapists turned teachers? How do you find out?

- Graduate placement help-- will they help you find a job, help you set up a practice?

- Is peer supervision available or do they teach you how to set up your own peer supervision group?

What type of learner are you and what style of teaching does a school offer?

Every person has a different learning style and each school has to be able to deal with different types of learners. The three learning types are:

Visual: learn by seeing information

Auditory: learn by hearing information

Kinesthetic: learn by doing or working through information

Walter McKenzie's online Multiple Intelligences Survey can help you learn more about what type of learner you are ("Multiple Intelligences Inventory").

Knowing what type of learner you are will help you in your learning experience at massage school. If you have difficulty understanding the subject or are not organized in your studying you can then go back to how you learn and find ways of learning that work best for you. Look for schools that make accommodations for different styles and provide teachers who can adapt and teach to your leaning style.

The location-- is it close and convenient?

The location of the school is important as you will be spending a lot of time there. Long distance driving takes time and money. How much time can you spend on the commute? The issue of travel to and from school may require a trade off – a school that has everything you want but is far away versus a school that has everything you need but is closer to home.

Class schedule -- are there evening or day-time hours and weekend classes-- hours that fit your schedule or can be made to fit?

Schools vary in the number of hours of training available. Often the number of hours in training is increased so that students can get financial aid in the form of federal grants and loans. The increased number of hours does not necessarily translate into a better massage school program or a better therapist. I have seen massage therapists graduate from 1,000 hour programs that are more lost and unsure of themselves than people graduating from 500 hour programs. But again, much really depends on the type of learner you are and your job hunting skills or business building skills.

Cost of classes-- is it within your budget?

The number of hours that you will choose will depend on the amount of money and time you have to invest in your training. It will also depend on your learning style, how motivated you are as a student and how much education you feel that you will need to be successful. Most massage therapists after graduation take additional continuing education classes to specialize in various types of massage or working with a specific health condition. Keith Grant, a massage school teacher and scientist, in his white paper on "A Review of Issues in Massage Governance" talks about the number of hours of education that are required to make a successful, competent massage therapist.

> "Educational research over the past 20-30 years compellingly demonstrates that learning in the classroom context often leads, not to usable understanding, but only to the ability to successfully answer test questions. Study after study has found that, by and large, even the best students in the best schools can't take knowledge learned in one setting and apply it appropriately in a different setting."

Being able to answer test questions and pass a test is different from being able to apply the information in a practice or job setting. A school that teaches with both in mind will provide a better educational experience.

The cost of massage school will vary depending on the number of hours of training the school provides. It can be anywhere from $3,000 to $30,000. When considering cost, you should keep in mind the salary statistics and the fact that it generally takes a few years to start a massage practice. Entry level jobs start at $12 an hour which will make paying back loans very difficult if not impossible. If you go into debt to go to massage school you will have to add that to your ability to make money right out of school so you can pay your bills. Some schools that offer federal financial aid options usually have longer programs. There are also some scholarships and grants to help pay for massage school but they are getting harder to find. Your massage school should be able to help you find more information about financial aid.

No matter what, as you decide on a school, cost can be a big factor. You may have to decide if going into debt will be worth it and at that time you should have a plan for paying the debt. If it is an option, you can save for massage school which will help when you graduate without any debt. Starting a business is generally expensive and will require that you have enough savings to live for a year or more until your business provides an adequate income. How you deal with these financial issues before massage school will affect your ability to be successful as a massage therapist when you start your new career.

The massage profession, more than most, seems to attract many people who have issues around money by saying that it isn't about the money, but frankly it is. You need money to live and pay the bills and to save for retirement. Many new therapists will say that they just want to help and subsequently sacrifice their own income so that they can help others.

Policies and procedures of schools-- what will you be responsible for and what will the school provide?

Another thing to look at is the school's policies and procedures so that you understand what is required and what the school will provide. The policies and procedures are basically the boundaries that keep the student safe and the teacher safe. Knowing what you are responsible for and what the school and teachers are responsible for will reduce problems while you are in school or after graduating. Boundaries about teacher-student dating or massage trades are important to maintain as those activities can negatively impact a student's ability to learn and to pass the school requirements.

The school must support the student with proper peer supervision. Peer supervision is a support system in which a more experienced massage therapist works with other massage therapists for the purpose of providing support. The primary purpose is actually to protect the best interests of the

client and work with the massage therapist on issues that often will have an impact on the ability to
be successful as a massage therapist. It can be
working with one peer supervisor or it can be
working with a group of your own peers guided by
a peer supervisor. The peer supervisor or peer
group will help by listening and offering feedback
on personal and professional challenges. (It isn't
someone telling you what to do as in regular supervision that you think of in work situations.) To
find out more about supervision see the later
chapter on peer supervision.

The school should have a graduate services department that teaches the student how to find a job or
set up a practice. Graduate services should also
have job listings and have job workshops to help
massage school graduates find jobs. They may also
have classes and support groups for starting and
running a business.

There are also other things to ask a potential massage school:

- What teaching qualifications do the instructors have? (Qualifications are items such as: experience in the field they are teaching, years of teaching a particular subject and specific training for either teaching or subject.)

- Do teachers have proper teaching credentials? (Credentials as in basic teaching skills.)

- Are the instructors recent massage school graduates? Many schools are using recent graduates without any teaching experience because of the recent large growth in the number of massage schools. Many do not have adequate teaching experience or credentials. (Whether the massage school will tell you honestly is a different matter, but you can ask.)

- How many graduates do they have that are practicing one year after graduating? Five years after graduating? Ten years after graduating? (Some accredited massage schools are required to collect those statistics so be sure to ask.)

- How many of the teachers have had or do have a massage practice? How many have worked full time in the profession? How many hours do they work in their practice or in a massage job? This is important as I see many massage schools hire massage therapists right out of massage school without any teaching background or work experience. Understanding what it takes to build a practice can help the massage teacher teach better and will also be able to set an example of a successful massage therapist. Not all teachers need to be massage therapists. People who teach science classes such as anatomy and pathology need to be aware of how these concepts will apply to someone learning massage. (As an entering student you need to know that you will get a wide range of teachers. But you hope that your chosen well established school has good standards and wants to do the best for you.)

There is a difference between learning just what you need to know to pass the school or state test and actually learning how to become a successful massage therapist. No matter what type of school you choose, it is ultimately up to you to put the effort you need into learning so that you can apply it adequately in a practice or massage job. There is a Massage School Questionnaire that will help you figure out what to ask when you visit massage schools in the resources section at the end.

The task of researching and choosing a massage school is very difficult because massage schools and associations often paint a rosy picture of careers in massage. I often wonder what the image of massage would be without all of the pictures in the massage school brochures and websites. What I see in a daily massage practice is nothing like the pictures with beautiful people getting a relaxing massage by a beautiful woman or a hunky male. I see clients with hairy backs, too stressed to lay still, scars, pain, various skin conditions, serious health issues, in wheelchairs, walking with canes –

none of which is the glamour that the ads portray. There are many very good schools that are able to balance making money with providing a solid education.

Curriculum and Hours

The number of hours and types of classes that each massage school offers varies greatly. The number of hours that are required by each state's massage board also varies somewhat but most require the basic 500 hours of training.

When I went to massage school in 1987, I was required to have 250 hours of training. The number of hours of training has constantly increased but for no clear reason. There has been little research or proof that it takes 500 hours of training to become a competent massage therapist. From what I have seen, the number of hours of training seems to have increased through the years mainly as a result of massage schools being able to get federal financial assistance for their massage students. Keith Eric Grants' "A Review of Issues on Massage

Governance" finds some support for that theory by saying:

> "There has been a sometimes not so subtle interplay between federal financial assistance programs and lobbying for particular hour requirements within state occupational regulation."

While the total number of hours in requirements may be the same, the actual number of hours in each specific class may vary from state to state, making it impossible for there to be reciprocity between states. You can't practice in any state just because you have a license in one state.

Most schools offer *more* than 500 hours of education without any proof that it is needed. Schools are of course able to make more money by offering longer classes. Many schools say that it will produce a more highly skilled massage therapist. More hours of training does not necessarily make for the best program. It really is more about the quality of the education hours. The number of hours of education you will need depends on how much you have to spend money and time-wise and what amount of education you need to feel comfortable about what you do. It will of course be difficult for you to know exactly since massage is new to you. Keep in mind that you will always be able to get help and support at any stage of your training and career to help you feel more confident in what you are doing.

You will also have to meet the requirements in the state where you want to work/live. A shorter course will allow you to get into the work force faster but you will lack experience. However you may be able to make it up by being an active learner when you get out of massage school or be willing to take lower paying jobs to get more experience. Longer classes are usually better for people who are right out of high school or need more time to build their confidence. There will always be more massage classes to take no matter what number of hours that you start out with. Continuing education is required in most states and most massages therapists like to learn more and more as they see the variety of issues their clients have.

Each state requires a specific number of hours of education in different topics such as anatomy, physiology, massage technique, pathology, business and ethics, and legal aspects. What is required by the National Certification Board or the Federation of State Massage Therapy Boards and what is required in your state may vary as far as course material.

For example:

The National Certification exam requires:

- A minimum of 500 hours of instruction as follows:
  125 hours of body systems (anatomy, physiology and kinesiology)
  200 hours of massage and bodywork assessment, theory and application, in-class and supervised

40 hours of pathology

10 hours of business and ethics (minimum of 6 hours in ethics)

125 hours of additional instruction in an area or related field that theoretically completes the massage program of study

- Graduate of a NCBTMB Assigned School Code with a current valid transcript submitted to NCBTMB

The Washington State Board of Massage requirements are different from the national requirements:

- 130 hours of anatomy, physiology and kinesiology including palpation, range of motion and physics of joint function. There must be a minimum of 40 hours of kinesiology.
- 50 hours of pathology, including indications and contraindications.
- 265 hours of theory and practice of massage to include techniques, remedial movements, body mechanics of the practitioner and the

impact of techniques on pathologies. A maximum of 50 of these hours may include time spent in a student clinic. Hydrotherapy is to be included when consistent with the particular area of practice.

- 55 hours of clinical/business practices minimally to include hygiene, record keeping, medical terminology, professional ethics, business management, human behavior, client interaction and state and local laws.

- Certification in American Red Cross first aid and American Heart Association Cardiopulmonary Resuscitation

- Four contact hours of training in HIV-AIDS in the following six topics: Etiology and epidemiology, Transmission and infection control, Testing and counseling, Clinical manifestations and treatment, Legal and technical issues, and Psychosocial issues. Training can be obtained from local community hospitals and colleges.

Even though the number of hours is the same (500), the actual class material required is different. You can see that the number of hours required for the various categories are different, meaning that you will have to comply with whatever your state requires. That is why you cannot just practice in any state that you want.

Many states also require that part of your training include a clinical rotation of actually working on clients either at the school or in a professional office space through an internship program. This allotted time is important in integrating the information you have learned and applying it to real life situations. It is important to find a school that takes their student clinic times seriously and to do as many massages as you can while in school to build your confidence for joining the workforce. Since so many massage schools offer evening and weekend clinic appointments, security is also an issue. Here are some things to consider:

- Do they have nicely lit, fully furnished clinical space?

- Is it in a safe area of town with security systems in place?

- Will there be a supervisor on the premises at all times during clinical hours to answer questions?

- What feedback will the supervisor give you? Are they allowed to or equipped to provide instruction about your techniques?

- Will you actually get one-on-one time with the supervisor each shift to talk about your clients and client experiences?

- Will you also have time with a group of students to talk about what you are experiencing?

- Will you have enough time to talk to clients and work with them?

- Will you have enough time in between client sessions to get ready for the next client and take care of your personal needs?

I have recently been aware of a number of high school students asking about massage school requirements. The American Massage Therapy Association and the Associated Bodywork and Massage Professional both say that the average age of a massage therapist is 45. Most massage schools have been geared toward adult learners. It has only been within the past 5-10 years, with the creation of massage franchises that offer more massage jobs that younger people right out of high school and those under 30 have found careers in massage more appealing. A two or four year massage program might be better for younger people just starting out in a career. Without any life or business experience, these students fill the low-paying jobs at the many massage franchises. There is even a chain of massage schools that are working exclusively with one of the major franchises for job placement. You have to remember though that entry level pay is usually around $12-$15 an hour at a massage franchise. With more experience and training, there are more possibilities for finding and creating higher-paying jobs.

Massage School is Science

Does a career in massage just mean giving a massage? Recent inquiries on my website – www.massage-career-guides.com – ask questions such as "Will I have to take math classes if I go to massage school?. The answer is "No, massage school does not require you to take math classes but you will be expected to keep up with science-based classes and basic college-level anatomy and physiology. Where you will really need to have basic math skills is after you graduate. You will need to be able to take care of your business accounts. That requires adding, subtraction and multiplication and of course, a good common business sense.

To perform a massage you need to understand how the body works, why massage works and how it works. The classes you take will be anatomy, physiology, pathology, massage theory, kinesiology (the study of muscles) and possibly even cadaver anatomy courses (yes! studying dead bodies). You will have to learn the muscles and bones of the body and how the other systems in the body are affected by massage. You will learn about kinesiology – how muscles move and what makes them work— and how to apply this to a massage. A course outline example is on my website (http://www.massage-career-guides.com/massage-school-notes.html) .

Massage School Teachers

Very few states regulate the requirements for Massage School instructors. The number of massage schools in 1985 was about 50 and now in 2011 there are at least 1,200 schools, a 2400% increase! With such an explosion in the massage school market, many schools are having a difficult time finding quality massage school teachers. To help meet the need for teachers, recent graduates are recruited into the teaching field. Unfortunately for the student, a recent massage practitioner will probably not be a good instructor or have any teaching experience. These new graduates may not have the experience of a full time practice, a business or have any experience working in the field.

While it is a great opportunity for massage graduates, the quality and/or experience of teaching assistants is not regulated and the result is less than ideal for the student and the massage profession. Just recently the Alliance for Massage Therapy Education has created a group for massage school teachers to help them learn to teach (http://www.afmte.org/online-training-center/).

Without regulations or schools for teaching massage instructors, the teaching profession is full of massage teachers who do not understand what it takes to have a full-time practice. While I am sure great schools and teachers exist, what I hear from people through my websites is that some teachers lack ethics such as in boundary skills and may date or become inappropriately friendly with students. These teachers are certainly not qualified to teach about boundaries to students. How to maintain boundaries is an important component in building a successful career in massage. Teachers must also be up to date with the latest research and information on massage and how it works. They must also know how to handle difficult student relationships and know how to actually teach. There also are some really amazing teachers out there that will help your career immensely. The trick is finding them.

The Associated Massage and Bodywork Professionals (AMBP) reports that because of the growing number of massage schools:

"One problem schools are facing is an insufficient number of qualified, experienced teachers to meet student demand. Explosive growth of 122.8 percent in schools and 107.1 percent in enrollment since 1998 has inevitably required the hiring of a disproportionate number of rookie instructors."

Choosing a Massage School

Making a final decision about massage school is a combination of what you need and what the school offers. Assuming you know what you need the following suggestions will help you choose a school:

Sit in on classes. Look at the environment, the size of the classrooms, the equipment, lighting, heating/cooling **systems**, libraries, resources, and student clinic.

Talk to the instructors in and out of class. Get a massage from the instructors if they practice somewhere.

Talk to the students. Ask them how they are doing, what they want to be doing when they graduate, what they think about the teachers and are they getting the support they need.

Talk to graduates of the school. Ask them if they liked the massage school. Did it prepare them to find a job or start a practice? Do they feel competent now that they are out in the workplace? Did they get what they needed from the massage school?

Talk to the school administrators. Ask them if they have any massage experience themselves? Why are they working at the school?

Get massages in the massage school's student clinics. Pay attention to how the students are treated and how they interact with the teachers. Ask the students how they like the program. Are they getting what they need?

Decide how much money you can spend and still have money to start your practice or hold you over until you find a job. Does the massage school have a program where you can pay over time? Do they have grants or scholarships that might help you?

Decide how much time you want to spend in massage school. Are you a fast learner? A self starter? Do you need more support in learning basic facts and massage techniques?

Take an introductory massage class. Most massage schools will offer a one day or weekend class. Going to one of these introductory classes will give you the experience of touching strangers. It can be difficult at first to touch strangers so taking a class like this will help you decide if you will be able to deal with touching others.

All of these activities will help provide information that will help you make a good decision. But in addition, don't forget that your intuition and how the school feels to you is a very important factor in choosing a school. In the meantime:

Get as many massages as you can from different massage therapists using different types of techniques. Ask massage therapists if they are making a decent living and how long it took them to do that. Ask them what school they went to or what additional classes they have taken. Do as much research as you can so that you can be well informed and make better choices for yourself.

Getting the most out of massage school

No matter which school you choose, there is a good chance that there will be some challenges and negative issues. No school or situation will be a perfect match. Every school has its drama and politics. Going to massage school to change your career can be a very stressful time. Your life will be spent studying, learning, practicing massage and trying to maintain your other life which may include work and family. Massage school also has a way of bringing out your most sensitive issues. Be ready and willing to learn about yourself!

I get many emails from students outlining their stressful school situations which include issues such as: massage school instructors not honoring their boundaries, dealing with poorly qualified teachers and not receiving the support the student expected to get. If any of these happen to you bring it to the school's attention. They can't fix it if they don't know about it. But in the meantime, stay focused on your goal of becoming a massage therapist by learning as much as you can. Make every effort to stay out of the drama.

You may run into misinformation being taught in school. This usually happens because research is just being done on massage and many of the things that are being taught as facts are just hearsay and passed on through teachers. For example, it was thought that working on people with cancer was contraindicated meaning that you should not do a massage on someone with cancer. It was thought that it would spread the cancer and cause it to metastasize in other areas of the body. With research and evidence it is now widely accepted that massage can help many people undergoing treatment for cancer. However, there are still schools that teach that it shouldn't be done. Another widely and continually debated topic is 'what happens to the body during massage?' Some people still say that massage releases toxins from the body when there is no scientific research showing that it does. Basic information about massage is changing so fast that it is difficult for some massage schools to keep up. Unfortunately there are no standardized state or national rules that make massage schools remain current with the latest information. While you are in school and something doesn't sound quite right ASK! Do more research on your own!

Help is on the way because there is now an organization called the <u>Alliance for Massage Therapy Education</u> that was created to make sure that massage schools are all teaching the same and current material. The Goals of the Alliance are to:

- Strengthen and improve massage education by providing information and educational opportunities to institutions, administrators, teachers and continuing education providers
- Provide forums for learning, fellowship and mutual support
- Advocate for the interests of members
- Serve as the designated representative for massage therapy education in dealing with other stakeholders in the field, as well as organizations and regulatory bodies outside the field
- Develop standards that guide and inform the effective teaching of massage therapy

- Promote access to massage therapy education to those who are seeking it, from entry-lovel training through post-graduate studios

While the Alliance and the Federation of Massage State Boards are working on improving massage education, it is just in the beginning stages of change so you are still on your own until the system improves.

You should also expect your school to abide by simple professional standards such as:

- Instructors must be punctual and teach for the full class. After all, you have paid for full instruction.
- Substitute teachers should be available if the primary teacher is not able to teach.
- Instructors should maintain professional standards such as not talking about students publically.
- Teachers should not be rude if they don't know the answer to your questions.

- Your teachers should know the licensing requirements in your state.

- Your tests should not be open book tests. Neither your final exams nor the state exam will be open book.

- Religion should not be a part of your massage curriculum.

- Go to all classes and be on time no matter what.

- Follow the teacher's instructions.

- Participate as much as you can by asking questions and voicing your feelings.

- Participate in peer supervision. If the massage school doesn't have a supervisor or peer group consider starting your own. Developing relationships with other students can help form a solid network when you graduate.

- Practice massage as much as you can. Get as many massages as you can from students, teachers and professionals. You learn just as much from receiving a massage as you do giving one really.

- If possible practice massage on teachers, you will get wonderful feedback.

- Get massages from teachers or other professionals and pay for those sessions. Paying creates a different dynamic than trading services and you will learn a lot from a massage given by experienced therapists.

- If you have a concern for your safety or have other touch issues like not wanting to be worked on by a man (whether you are a man or woman), bring them to the attention of your teachers and get help with bringing your concerns out. It is important to learn about these issues personally but also because you may have clients in the future who have similar issues.

- Get as much help and attention from the teachers as you can.

- If you have a problem with the school bring it to the school's attention. If the school does not respond in a satisfactory manner contact your state board.

- While in school start planning and researching your future work. Begin investigating jobs or areas to set up your business. Save money so that you will be able to pursue your dream job or dream practice.

- Find a mentor to encourage you while you are in school and later when you are out of school and starting on your new career.

Massage School should be a fun and exciting time in your life. Taking care of yourself while you make such big changes in your life is one of the first steps to becoming a successful massage therapist. It will set the stage for your career so try to get the most out of the experience by putting all that you can into it.

Chapter 8.
A Job in Massage
or Your Own Business?

As a massage therapist you will have many options about where you want to work, whether as an employee or starting your own business. You don't need to decide immediately, but it is a good idea to start thinking about it so you can plan financially and otherwise. While most massage therapists do start their own practice, starting as an employee can help you learn the ropes and learn how to start and run a massage business. It is also possible to start out as an employee at a massage franchise like Massage Envy and work your way up to higher paying jobs at other clinics or facilities.

There are so many opportunities in this profession that the sky really is the limit. This section gives you some ideas to start you thinking about what you want and to find out more about what the possibilities really are.

Jobs In Massage

Jobs in massage are becoming more and more available every day. When I finished massage school in 1987, there were very few jobs and most of those jobs were as an independent contractor, which really means that you were self-employed. The new popularity of massage has created many new positions but it has also created new problems. Many employers are not massage therapists themselves therefore they may not understand how massage works or what a massage therapist needs in order to provide the best service. Many employers also are in it for the money, which is fine considering it is a business, but it is contradictory to many massage therapist's reasons for becoming a massage therapist. They often say: "It isn't about the money". If you decide to work for someone else for a while here are some items that are necessary for success:

1. Does the position pay enough money to provide for your needs?

2. Are there enough clients scheduled so that you can make the promised amount of money?

3. Are benefits such as sick and vacation pay, health insurance and retirement plans available as part of the job?

4. Is there enough time between sessions to change linens and comfortably get each client in and out of the room?

5. Do they do chart notes on clients so that you can track each client and be more efficient when working with new people?

6. Is there enough time to do a thorough client interview and take notes and also do chart notes on each client?

7. Are there scheduled breaks and lunch hours?

8. Are the hours reasonable so that you can take care of your body and reduce the chance of physical injury?

9. Will you be learning about getting and keeping clients or involved in the process of marketing and doing business?

10. Is there a support group that will help you mentally/emotionally/ spiritually be successful?

11. Do you feel your work will be valued and respected by your employer?

Finding an employer who understands that you are a part of what will make their business successful and are willing to train you in the many aspects of running a business can help you be more successful in your career. Be clear about your needs and set goals to find the job that meets your criteria. Since you will be new to the massage job market, it may mean taking a few jobs to earn money and also to learn more about what you really want. The challenge is to do that while paying the bills and exploring the many possibilities. Every job is an opportunity for learning and growth.

But first, you really need to know exactly what you need to earn. You can do that by doing an inventory of your living expenses, including taxes (if you are an independent contractor you will have to set aside 15% for self-employment tax), vacations funds, emergency funds, savings, retirement funds and insurance costs. Knowing what you need will help you make a better decision when it comes to taking a massage therapy job. Know what benefits you need and what hours you want to work. Create a vision of your ideal job in massage and then when looking at employment possibilities see if they match your vision. When you take a job that is less than your ideal job you need to be aware that the chances that it will be draining on you increase significantly. You will need more self care tools and work towards doing what you need to do to get a job that fills your vision of an ideal job.

One of the best ways that massage therapists can find a job they want is to get a massage at the place you may be thinking of applying to. As you get the massage ask questions. Notice how you are treated in every way. Are you rushed in and out? Does the therapist handle the money transaction her/him-self? Are the linens clean and is the environment appealing? Is there a well-appointed waiting room? How is your first call for your appointment? Are they friendly and efficient? How do they ap-pear when you visit? Is everyone standing around the front desk talking about the fact that the bath-room needs cleaning or is everyone engaged in their jobs? Visiting many massage establishments before you even go to massage school may also help you decide whether you really want to be a massage therapist after all. Often discovering what you need is often a process of discovering what you don't like. Make sure you write your impressions down so that later you can remember accurately when you are ready to compare or apply. Create a file of all the schools you are looking at and keep a list of your questions that come up.

There are also places to research that may not currently have massage employees. Many hospitals, nursing homes and assisted living places are just starting to hire massage therapists. Many corporations now have wellness centers with chair and even full table massage so that their employees can have access to massage by appointment during work.

But knowing what you want always comes first.

- How much money do you need to make each week/month?
- What days and hours do you want to work?
- What type of massage do you want to be doing? Relaxation? Deep Tissue? Treatment or clinical massage work?
- What are you able to supply to do your work? Massage oils/lotions? A Massage table? Other supplies? What do you want the management to be responsible for?
- How will you be paid? Are hours that you spend not doing massage paid at the same rate as when you are doing a massage?

- What benefits do you need? Health insurance for you and/or your family? Vacation? Retirement accounts?

- What incentives are there for you to promote massage and bring in clients of your own?

- What happens when you want to leave? Will you be able to set up an office or work near the place? Some places will make you sign non-compete clauses that are very controversial. Even though employers want to keep clients after you leave, clients will often follow the massage therapist.

- Who is responsible for the client files? If you are doing insurance work, you may be responsible for keeping client files for a few years or more.

- Do you want to be a regular employee where the employer pays you benefits and pays a portion of your taxes?

- Do you want to be an independent contractor and basically work for yourself but have someone helping you get clients? An independent contractor will pay their own taxes and be able to set their own hours.

With any job and particularly massage therapy jobs, it is important to have your role clarified and written up in a contract so there is no question when situations arise. The process of getting a written agreement will also tell you a lot about the employer.

Massage therapy jobs are often set up as a subcontractor or independent contractor position which is really the same as being self-employed. A chiropractor or other business will hire massage therapists to do massage on a contract basis. The business owner usually will provide clients for the massage therapist. The massage therapist will usually also be responsible for getting clients. It is often difficult to determine if you are an employee or an independent contractor. It is cheaper for the employer to hire independent contractors but many times massage therapists should really be a true employee. It is up to the employer to make the correct determination, but many massage therapists are still being taken advantage of by employers. After taking a class by two attorneys hired by the American Massage Therapy Association of Washington State, I learned that if the business owner wants to pay you a percentage of the fee, then you should be classified as an employee and be paid employee benefits and the employer should pay labor and industry fees (unemployment fund). You would be considered an employee on commission. Many chiropractors and other business owners will try to set it up as a sub-contractor position which means you are responsible for your own self-employment taxes which is a considerable amount more (15% compared to about 7% you pay as an employee - the employer pays the rest). While I am not a lawyer, I think it is important for you to clarify your position and hire a lawyer to help you do so if you have any questions. There is more information on the IRS Website and a form that the employer can fill out to have the IRS determine the status of the position. It is the employer's responsibility to know this, as they will be responsible for the taxes and fees. The massage professional associations have yet to help clarify this situation so chiropractors and others continue to take advantage of massage therapists. You are really on your own when determining your status as an employee or independent contractor.

You can get more info that will help you start the process to determine your status at the following website:

http://massagepracticebuilder.com/massage-independent-contractors.

Here is a brief overview of what types of jobs are available and what kind of places hire massage therapists:

- Massage franchises
- Day spas, medical spas or destination spas
- Salons
- Health clubs, gyms, fitness centers
- Chiropractors, dentists, physical therapists, doctors
- Sports teams, clubs and associations
- Chair massage

- Hospitals, nursing homes, assisted living communities
- Cruise ships

Massage Franchises such as Massage Envy, Elements and Hand and Stone are creating a new business concept for the massage profession. They offer inexpensive massage through a membership program where clients pay a low monthly fee of $39-$59 per month. The clients receive one massage a month and usually have options to purchase other massages for themselves and family. Working at a massage franchise can be a good way to gain experience because the franchises can be very busy. Hands-on experience will help your career. The problem is that therapists only earn $12-$15 an hour. Since each location is independently owned there is a wide variation in the people that run each franchise and the salary and benefits that they offer. Many are giving the massage profession a bad image by paying massage therapists low wages with no benefits and having them do back-to-back massages without a break. Working long shifts and low pay can increase the amount of stress on your body and increase your chances of injury or burnout. Working for less than you need to make can be draining emotionally as well as financially. Because of the physical demands of the work, it is important to take care of yourself and understand what you need. Just like everything else, it is a matter of creating boundaries that support you in your process. You will need to have basic relaxation massage skills and also deep tissue and pregnancy massage training. It will also be helpful to take chair massage classes.

Spas come in many different shapes and forms offering hydrotherapy services, massages and facials. You will probably need extra training in spa therapies and also may need additional licensing to do skin care treatments. Some spas will teach how to do the treatments on site as part of your employee training. There are many different types of spas and massage job situations at spas. There is also a wide range of salaries and benefits and work situations. There are schools that offer special classes in spa therapies.

For more information see:
"Choosing the Spa That's Best for You"
<http://www.massagemag.com/spa/treatment/choose.php>.

"Battleground Conditions in the Spa: Gearing up for Work in a Tough Industry"
<http://www.massageandbodywork.com/Articles/OctNov2005/Battleground.html>.

Salons (beauty and nail salons) also offer massage therapists a place to work. However, some issues that go along with working in salon are toxic smells from hair and nail treatments and noise from the equipment. You may be able to rent space at a salon and start your own business. You will also have a client base of people who know the salon giving you a good chance of success.

Health clubs are a great place to start your career in massage as health club members often already have an interest in health. Massage is a great adjunct to working out and can be very beneficial for strength building and endurance training. Watch out for noisy aerobics classes and loud music right next to the massage room! You will most likely need training in sports massage, injury prevention and working with various medical conditions.

Chiropractors hire many massage therapists as employees or subcontractors. They also seem to have the lion's share of bad publicity for some of their less-than-ideal hiring practices. While massage and chiropractic treatments are very complimentary in the loosening of muscles before an adjustment, chiropractors often limit the amount of time for a session with sessions averaging 15-30 minutes. Chiropractors may try to bill a higher fee than most full massage sessions and pay you very little of it in return. They are notorious for not wanting to hire employees and provide benefits. In this situation also you must know what you need and want or you may become resentful of the chiropractor. I have received many emails from

people complaining about their situations but fail-
ing to see that they agreed to the arrangement in
the beginning. Be sure to clarify your agreement
before accepting work. Know what the chiropract-
or will be billing the insurance/client and what
they will be paying you per session. You might also
be able to rent an office from a chiropractor and
build a good working relationship. Chiropractors
are a good source of clients. You will need classes
in working with injuries, especially those associated with car accidents such as whiplash and other
trauma.

Doctors, dentists and other medical professionals
are now hiring massage therapists to work in different capacities. Dentists are using massage to
help relax the patients and also to help with jaw
problems. This usually involves doing massage
work in the mouth (with protective gloves on of
course!). You will need to be aware of any laws in
your state around working in the mouth. Some
states prohibit it while others require extra training. You can still do effective work by working out-

side the mouth. Physical therapists and occupational therapy offices hire massage therapists to do the massage part of the session. Doctors, especially naturopaths or holistic doctors, are realizing the value of massage and hiring them or renting space out to massage therapists. You can benefit from taking classes in working with various health conditions such as fibromyalgia, back and neck pain, herniated discs or other musculoskeletal conditions. Learning how to read and interpret research will also be beneficial when working with doctors and the medical profession. You will also need to have good charting skills to track sessions for insurance and for your own benefit and may need to know about billing insurance.

Professional and amateur sports teams hire massage therapists to work on team members and even travel with the team. In some states, you do not need to be licensed as a massage therapist to work with the athletes if you are a trainer for the team. Massage is really effective for helping to enhance athletic performance and to reduce injury. It is also very helpful in reducing the time of recovery from injury, allowing the athlete to get back to training or their competition. You can work with every sport from dancers, football, soccer, tennis, baseball, golf, basketball, track and field and more. You can work with professional athletes, amateurs, master's athletes and just the weekend athlete. Expect long hours, erratic schedules and working with people who are really hard on their bodies especially when working with professional athletes. Amateur athletes or people who just are physically active need regular massage to keep them going also. There are special sports massage classes that will teach you about working with athletes prior to events and after their events along with dealing with injuries and working to prevent injuries.

On site massage (chair massage) is also becoming a popular setting for massage. Airports, office buildings and convention centers are setting up chair massage kiosks where clients can get short back, neck and arm/hand massages. Clients do not have to get undressed which may make it attractive to those with a tight schedule or touch issues.

David Palmer is credited with starting the massage chair phenomenon but the "Massage Bar" has taken it even a step farther by creating a million-dollar airport and convention center business. Chair massage is even being offered in natural grocery stores such as Whole Foods (see www.mymassagecorner.com).

Chair massage can also be used to market your business setting up at health fairs, festivals or just about anywhere. Chair massage classes are really specific classes that will teach you how to do a seated massage with the clothing on. Learning chair massage can help you in building your business.

Hospitals, nursing homes, hospice and assisted living communities are also hiring massage therapists. There is a hospital massage network that you can join online at:

http://www.naturaltouchmarketing.com/HBMN-hospital-massage/HBMNHome.php

Be aware that working with patients will require special skills. A good knowledge of pathology and contraindication is a must. You will be working with people in various stages of aging and dying and will be faced with the issues that go along with working with that population. You will need extra training in the pathologies that go along with aging and have an understanding of the aging process.

For more information see:
"The Challenges and Rewards of Hospice Massage"
<http://www.massagemag.com/Magazine/2005/issue116/Hopice.php>

Working on a cruise ship may also seem attractive to a massage therapist. The ability to travel and do massage in a relaxing environment may be a good match for a massage therapist. You can find routine cruise lines with just the usual travel destinations but also cruises that are oriented to fitness, health and personal growth. You may have better luck working for a cruise line that offers cruises focused on an aspect of getting healthy. In general, the hours may be long and you may feel trapped on the boat with your clients. Your off time is spent resting to prepare for another full day of doing massage. But again it is really just a matter of setting boundaries at your job. You usually live for free on the boat and get to see many interesting places. You can benefit from taking spa type massage classes and general relaxation massage. For more information on working on a cruise ship:

Steiner Leisure – Trains and hires massage therapists for cruise ships.
<http://www.steinerleisure.com/main/Page.aspx?PageID=5000>

"Cruise Industry Employment: The Pros & Cons"
<http://www.massagetherapy.com/articles/index.php/article_id/585/Cruise-Industry-Employment>

Expert advice from *Massage Magazine* on getting a cruise ship job.

<http://www.massagemag.com/Magazine/2001/issue89/advice89.php>

Many, many massage job possibilities and opportunities exist. No matter what path you choose, working as a massage employee requires that you participate and take responsibility for yourself and your work. The challenge is setting boundaries to support you in your work and career path. As a massage employee you actually do have a lot of responsibility in creating your own future and the success of the business you are working for. Clients will come back because of you – they will also not come back because of you. Knowing this and participating fully in your work will make your chances of success at a massage job much greater.

Working for someone else can give you a lot of hands-on experience and an opportunity to learn the business side of massage. You can use a job in massage to supplement your family income or to make a full time living. There are many places that will provide higher paying jobs with good benefits. The challenge will be to say NO to low paying jobs without benefits or less-than-ideal work situations while you hold out for a better job or take a less-than ideal job while you look. It can even take a few years before you find that ideal massage job but it can be done with patience and perseverance.

Some of the things to look for in a job in massage are:

- Adequate hourly wages – in my opinion, $25 or more an hour are a must.
- Is there sick pay, vacation pay, health insurance and retirement funding?
- Is there money for continuing education, licensing and liability insurance?
- Is there adequate time in between sessions to change the table and talk to clients?
- Is there time allotted to do a thorough intake with each client so that you can know more about what they need?
- Is there support and guidance in getting and keeping clients?
- Can you get help with your massage skills, customer service skills?

- Are there opportunities to learn about the business and participate in marketing and management?

- Look for places that do not make you sign a non-compete clause. A client should be able to get a massage where ever they want and you should be able to work where ever you want to work.

- Finding or creating a niche for yourself like specializing in a specific technique like structural integration or cranial-sacral therapy for example or specialize in working with a specific health condition like fibromyalgia or carpal tunnel can help set you apart from all of the other massage therapists out there looking for a job.

In summation, this really is about learning to set boundaries for yourself and being able to say no when you are treated badly. Employers may have their own problems and may be under stress or just do not really understand what it takes for a massage therapist to do their job effectively. When jobs are scarce, massage therapists may take jobs that are less than ideal as a stepping stone in their career. As I have stated many times, many business owners are not massage therapists so they may not really understand that you are the reason for their success. It is your massage skill and your ability to connect with clients that will keep clients coming back and will get clients to refer their friends. It is important to educate the employers and stand up for what you need to do your work effectively. While saying no can be difficult when you have bills to pay, remember that there are many job opportunities in massage. You may have to or even want to take a low paying job to start with to get more experience.

Recently, there have been suggestions of unionizing massage therapists. I personally don't think that it would be a good solution to the problems therapists face, but think that it is necessary for massage therapists to be able to stand up for themselves. The answer lies in each therapist learning to create boundaries, finding or creating their ideal job and by following their passion.

After you graduate there is another book that I have about creating or getting your ideal massage job:

The Massage Job Guide – How to find or create higher paying jobs in massage.

http://www.massage-career-guides.com/massage-therapy-jobs.html

The following is an excerpt from Napoleon Hill's
Think and Grow Rich Formula for Jobs

First - Decide exactly what kind of job you want. If the job doesn't already exist, perhaps you can create it.

Second - Choose the company or individual that you wish to work with.

Third - Study your prospective employer as to policies, personnel, and chances of advancement.

Fourth - By analysis of yourself, your talents and capabilities, figure out WHAT YOU CAN OFFER, and plan ways and means of giving advantages, services, developments, or ideas that you can successfully deliver.

Fifth - Forget about "a Job". Forget whether or not there is an opening. Forget the usual routine of "have you got a job for me? Concentrate on what you can give.

Sixth - Once you have your plan in mind, arrange with an experienced writer to put it on paper in neat form and in full detail.

Seventh - Present it to the proper person with the authority and he/she will do the rest. Every company is looking for people who can give something of value, whether it is ideas, services, or connections. Every company has room for the man who has a definite plan of action which is to the advantage of that company.

Starting Your Own Massage Business

Most massage therapists at one time or another will start their own massage business. Starting your own business means that you will be taking responsibility for all aspects of the business: book-keeping, marketing, receptionist, massage therap-ist and janitor. You will have to find a location for your massage business and set up a business plan to follow to keep you on track. When you start your own business you will have much more con-trol over the massages you do and the hours that you work. It also means that you will be respons-ible for getting clients on the table and for making the money that you need to stay in business along with paying yourself the salary that you need. There are more opportunities for growth and ex-pansion when you start your own business.

Massage Home Business: Many massage ther-apists are drawn by the prospect of having their own business and setting it up in their home. It cuts down the costs of doing business but also al-lows you to attend to children or family life. The downside of working out of your home is that you will have strangers in your house. A separate massage room, bathroom and entrance would be preferable, but is not always doable. You will be faced with the challenges of keeping your family life and business life separate and by having to keep your house clean and presentable. Pets may be a problem for clients because of allergies and being afraid of animals. There is an increased risk of security when you work on clients in your home because you are basically letting strangers into your home. There are ways to stay safe and keep your home life separate from your work life and successfully work out of your home.

Mobile Massage Business: Another popular massage business is outcall massage where you go into people's homes, hotels or other locations. This may be appealing because of the low overhead in starting the business. You just need a massage table, a way to get to the clients' location and a phone for them to contact you. However, you will have travel expenses along with having to carry all of your tools –table and supplies– to each location. If you have a vehicle that can accommodate all those tools it is an easy way to get to work. You will soon learn that some people's homes are less than ideal for setting up a massage table and even getting the table into the room designated for the massage can be a challenge. I once carried a bulky massage table and all my massage supplies, up two flights of stairs through a narrow hallway each time I had to give a massage.

Going into people's homes and hotel rooms can also be a security issue. You can choose to only go to locations where you know the people or have been referred by people you trust. You can also set up a security system to let people know where you are and when you come and go. Be aware that when you travel to client's homes or to hotels you will need to charge extra for travel time. It is very convenient for clients to have a massage at home and most will gladly pay extra. You can specialize and focus on high end hotels or resort areas. You can also set parameters like only going to a location when there are two or more clients getting a massage on the same day.

While working out of your home or doing outcall massage may be appealing and looks to have less risk than taking on the expenses of overhead, it can be much more difficult than renting an office space. There are many options for renting an office space that can make it affordable. It is often a scary experience to rent a space when you don't have any clients, but you will need to trust in yourself and your chosen career.

You can always rent space from another massage therapist or health care provider so that you don't have to take on the expense of starting a business. You can also start with the home or mobile massage business and work your way up to getting your own office. You will have to spend money to rent an office, set it up and advertise and market your massage practice. You must look at it as an investment in your business and not just a business expense. You will have to spend some money to make money.

That being said, I do know successful massage therapists who do have their massage business in their home or doing strictly hotel/resort outcall massage. It is just a matter of doing what is right for you.

More information is available through the online article listed below:

"Outcall Service and Safety: Preparation is the Key to Success"
http://www.massageandbodywork.com/Articles/JuneJuly2000/outcall.html

Massage Office: There are many ways to set up your massage business. You can rent space from another massage therapist or other health care provider such as an acupuncturist or chiropractor for a few days a week or you can jump in with both feet and rent an office space on your own. If the space is large enough and has several treatment rooms you can rent out rooms to other practitioners. You can also set up a massage business and hire therapists, paying them employee wages and benefits or hire them as independent contractors. Each of these choices have risks and benefits. Again, it really depends on what you want and how good your business skills are more than your ability to do massage.

Here is a short list of the things you will have to do, learn and be responsible for when you set up a massage office:

- Proper massage and business licensing and permits.
- Find and rent an office space. Sign contract for renting month to month or short or long term lease.
- Buy and set up office equipment such as telephone, fax machine, computer, desk, chairs, waiting room chairs, end tables, lamps, wall art and decorations. The massage room will require massage table, sheets, pillows, bolsters, linens, music system, and decorations. In addition, clients must have access to a bathroom and if possible a shower and dressing room.

- Office policies such as fees, cancellation and no-show policies and a method for enforcing them.

- An office phone system to take appointments and/or use an online appointment system. An answering service or a method for accepting and recording calls.

- An accounting and billing system and a good accountant to help you file taxes.

- An insurance billing system with proper forms and paperwork for billing insurance (if you plan on going into that work).

- Advertising and marketing which ranges from creating a website to building a referral network of other health care professionals to joining the chamber of commerce.

- Continuing education classes to learn about customer service and customer problem solving as well as business and marketing.

Having your own office means you will have more control over your hours and your practice but it also means you will be doing everything that a business requires. The process will be a challenging but it can also be very rewarding. There are many resources such as books and websites as well as coaches and supervisors to help you. If you have the funds and especially if you don't like doing that part of the work, you can hire help for the marketing, website development and accounting. I also recommend that you hire a business coach and supervisor or join a peer group to get the support that you need in starting and running a business. You don't have to do it alone!

Chapter 9.
Self Care

After nearly 24 years of being a massage therapist, I can truthfully say that it is more about taking care of yourself than taking care of clients. Self-care is often thought of as all of those things you do to take care of yourself on the outside – getting regular massage, resting and taking vacations, taking time in between clients, practicing yoga or other movement therapies, good body mechanics at the massage table and eating the proper foods. While these are an important part of staying healthy and injury free in a profession that is demanding of the body, these things are only a part of good self-care.

Self-care also includes how you take care of yourself emotionally, mentally and spiritually. It is also how you set boundaries for yourself to support your business financially. Good self-care builds self-esteem, self-confidence and self-awareness. With those in place, you can increase your chances of success.

Cidalia Paiva in her book *"Keeping the Professional Promise"* states:

> "Health care practitioners must remember that the greatest gift we offer our clients, apart from our knowledge and skills, is our presence. The person we bring to the therapeutic relationship is an extremely important part of the healing process. A healthy, positive presence can and will enable the therapist to facilitate healing while an unhealthy, unfocused inattentive presence can create the opposite result: a failure to provide a therapeutic outcome or, worse still, the client's presenting condition can become aggravated or exacerbated.... Healthy self esteem is a vital part of what the therapist should bring to the therapeutic relationship."

While many massage therapists are drawn to the massage profession by thinking they want to help others, helping happens to be one of the biggest causes of burnout in the massage profession. The desire to help may have hidden agendas that come from unconscious beliefs and patterns. Therapists may think that by helping others they will feel good about themselves. They think that by helping others they make their lives more meaningful. The problem begins when massage therapists start giving up their own needs for the sake of fulfilling the needs of others. This shows up in many different ways:

- Charging less than you need to make.
- Taking jobs that pay you less than you need to make.
- Taking jobs that drain you more than support you.
- Working on clients that drain you more than nurture you.
- Giving more of your time than you charged for (like doing an hour and a half massage

for an hour session "because they needed it").

- Giving discounts that you can't really afford.

- Excessive volunteering and giving too many free massages.

- Not charging for latecomers or no-shows or last minute cancellations.

- Repetitive stress injuries or other health issues such as chronic fatigue.

- Burnout.

- Ineffective marketing.

- Thinking that doing massage is about fixing clients and that you are the only one who can do that!

- Thinking that you have to work on everyone that calls or walks in the door.

- Feeling that you gave everything and tried everything and were not appreciated.

- Saying things like 'it isn't about the money'.

- Saying that you don't need much money, claiming 'Noble Poverty" as Mikelann Valterra talks about in her book *Women and Underearning*.

- The idea that your needs are less important than those of others makes you feel good.

Being a good massage therapist requires that you take care of yourself. Learning takes time and energy and if all your energy is used on others you will quickly stagnate.

You often hear massage therapists and students say: "I am not doing this for the money". Many are brought to the massage profession after having a serious injury or chronic pain and experiencing relief from massage after a long process of traditional therapy. They may want to give to others what was given to them. While it is okay to want to help others, the very things that may lead you to seek out a massage career may also be the things that may eventually lead to your leaving that career. This is one of the main reasons for seeking supervision – to help you to become aware of your helping patterns and learn how to set boundaries to support you.

The truth is money is important and anyone who says it isn't will most likely find themselves out of business and out of a career. A business needs money to survive. A therapist needs money to live. It takes money to continue learning and growing. The money you earn may pay the bills but you also need it to take of yourself so that you can care for others.

Rarely do massage therapists even think of making $100,000 a year or more. Why? Because of the misguided belief that money is not important to the 'real' massage therapist. Massage schools may inadvertently encourage that belief by telling new graduates "don't quit your day job" or "massage is a good part-time career", which implies that a career in massage can't support you. Not true! However, as a profession we need to start addressing those beliefs by changing the image of the 'starving massage therapist' to the 'wealthy massage therapist'.

The desire of 'wanting to help others' is often filled with hidden agendas. There is a big difference between helping and being of service. When you help others it often implies that someone is incapable of supporting themselves. It creates a difference in power. Dr. Rachel Remen says it best in her article "In the Service of Life":

> "Serving is different from helping. Helping is based on inequality; it is not a relationship between equals. When you 'help' you use your own strength to help those of lesser strength. If I'm attentive to what's going on inside of me when I'm helping, I find that I'm always helping someone who's not as strong as I am, who is needier than I am. People feel this inequality. When we 'help' we may inadvertently take away from people more than we can ever give them; we may diminish their self-esteem, their sense of worth, integrity and wholeness. When I 'help' I am very aware of my own strength. But, we don't serve with our strength, we serve with ourselves. We draw from all of our experiences."

Because clients come to us for 'help' and we are taught to 'fix' in massage school, unconscious parts of ourselves will come up in our practice. This will happen whether you want them to or not, whether you are aware of them or not and whether you are willing to look at them or not. In order to be of service to others one must learn about what drives the need to 'help'. This isn't an easy or one-step process but more of a lifelong search that can often be addressed through supervision and peer supervision groups.

An answer to the 'needing to help' issue is that you may be trying to take care of others in the way you yourself need or needed to be taken care of. I call this phenomenon "The Code of the Caretaker". Gerald and Marianne Corey talk about this in their book "*Becoming a Helper*":

> "Because helpers ask clients to examine their behavior to understand themselves more fully, we ask helpers to be equally committed to an awareness of their own lives."

They further state: "It is critical that you be honest with yourself about the needs you will satisfy by entering this field. Your motives and needs can work for you or against both you and your future clients." Although they are referring to the psychology profession, I think it really applies to the massage profession also and anyone in any helping profession.

Jack Blackburn, a Trager practitioner and peer supervision advocate in Seattle, describes the difference between caretaking and caregiving as:

> "When we care-take we assume responsibility for our clients' healing. When we care-give we support clients in assuming responsibility for their own healing."

Part of the problem is that caretaking is often an unconscious action. The roots of caretaking come from early childhood and how our individual needs were met as infants and children. Caretaking may often develop as a defense mechanism. We may care-take to assure that we are not rejected or judged. We care-take because we need to be needed. We care-take thinking we are helping others. The line between caretaking and caregiving is not always black and white. Because the role of the massage therapist involves people who are seeking help from the massage therapist and helping others has a way of making both parties feel good (at least temporarily), it is important that the massage therapist understand that the 'care-taking' issue can be a very big one. Therapists need to be aware that peer supervision or peer group support can really work to help the process of becoming more conscious of the patterns and beliefs of 'helping' and building a successful career.

You can find more information online in the following articles:

Jack Blackburn. Series of articles on Caretaking and Supervision:< Presencingsource.com>

Diane Polseno. "Enabling: The Dark Side of Helping":<http://www.amtamassage.org/uploads/cms/documents/ethically_speaking.pdf>

Rick Goggins . "Ergonomics for MTs and Bodyworkers":
<http://www.massageandbodywork.com/Articles/FebMar2007/ergonomicsformts.html>

Chapter 10.
Supervision, Peer Supervision, Mentoring.

Peer supervision, peer supervision groups and mentoring are only recently becoming available in the massage profession. One of the tools that can help you learn about your issues around 'helping' as well as support you in building your career is peer supervision and mentoring. It can also an important part in building a successful practice.

The process of supervision and the relationships that arise from it, can be helpful in learning how to apply what you learned in massage school into building a massage practice or finding your ideal massage therapy job. All that you learned in massage school about anatomy, physiology, pathology and massage are really just the beginning – you need to know how to put it all together and create a successful career -either start a business or find a job.

Supervision - Supervision isn't the kind of supervision you see in typical work settings. This definition of supervision comes from the psychology profession. Supervision describes a relationship with a more experienced massage therapist (or counselor) for the purpose of exploring the therapeutic relationship or issues around being a massage therapist. It requires looking at the core issues of why and how we help, how we feel about clients and many other problems that arise during the course of being in business as a massage therapist. The role of the supervisor is to just listen. Yes, just listen. However, the supervisor may lead you to the answers by asking questions that facilitate the process of looking at your career and things that come up on a daily basis. A supervisor generally does not give advice but rather listens and reflects back to the massage therapist what they hear the massage therapist is really saying. This process assists the therapist to become more aware of his or her role in the therapeutic process and enhances the opportunities for healing. When I first heard the word "supervision", I immediately thought that I didn't want anyone telling me what to do! Peer Supervision is definitely not that! I hope in the future the term supervision will be changed to eliminate confusion.

Peer Supervision Groups- Peer supervision groups are groups of massage therapists who meet regularly to discuss the issues of the therapeutic relationship and whatever comes up on a daily basis in their practice. It is usually a group of eight people or less and can be a minimum of three people. A supervisor may join the group at the beginning to teach the process of active listening and to provide further insights. Each member gets a chance to share experiences and receive feedback from the group.

In supervision, you may talk about the issues that come up on a daily basis in the course of working as a massage therapist. This process allows you to look at the reasons why 'you charge less than you need to make 'or 'don't enforce a cancellation policy'. The group process can be whatever you need it to be and is closely related to mentoring. You can get assistance with any and all aspects of your career.

Mentoring - Mentoring describes a relationship between two massage therapists for the purpose of _sharing information_ needed to build and sustain a massage business. It is usually between a massage therapist who is just starting their business and a massage therapist who has been in the business for awhile. Mentoring is another avenue used to teach a person about the business of massage. It can include information on insurance billing, bookkeeping, marketing, techniques, how to deal with clients, etc.

Mentoring can help in all the steps one needs to take as a massage therapist. A mentor can show you how to set your fees, talk to clients, market your business and learn to bill insurance.

Peer supervision and mentoring are just starting to become part of the massage profession. A massage school with a peer supervision and mentoring program would be an ideal situation. If the school you are considering does not have one, it is recommended that you start one yourself and get the support that you need. You can find more information about starting a group on my website at www.massage-career-guides.com

Chapter 11.
A Career in Massage –
Is it for you?

The decision to become a massage therapist rests with you. It has little to do with the massage itself or anything you learn in massage school. It has little to do with your age, situation, ethnicity or abilities. Your success in this or any other career depends on the amount of self-esteem and self-confidence you have and your ability to learn about yourself. It is about your *commitment* to being successful. The search for a fulfilling career is usually a mirror for the search for ourselves. In his book "Diamond Heart: Book One, " A. H. Almaas says:

"Your career, interests, relationships are very important – but they are only important insofar as they lead you toward a deeper understanding of yourself. Otherwise they are irrelevant."

There are so many different paths that you can take in massage that your career options are unlimited. There are many different arenas – one for people following a more technical path, one for people following the body/mind connection and still another for people pursing energy work. There are also many combinations in-between. You can pursue the path of spa massage which focuses on relaxation, stress reduction and pampering. If one path doesn't work out for you, you can always switch!

You can be employed at a spa, franchise or medical office or you can start your own business. You can work on a cruise ship or at a chair massage station in an airport. You can approach businesses with a plan to help them improve their business through the reduction of stress and pain. You can set up a chair massage business at a truck stop or at an assisted living center. You can specialize in working with pain syndromes and injuries or in medically oriented businesses.

The possibilities are unlimited. What may limit you are your beliefs about success and money. Learn about yourself and your feelings about success and set up indicators so that you will know when you have achieved that success. You can make as much or as little money as you want as long as you get what you need to function well.

What makes the difference between someone who is successful in this business and someone who ends up leaving due to an injury or lack of clients is the commitment you have in making it work for you. It is about having the patience and persistence to follow your dream. It is about learning about yourself and growing with your career.

Your decision is not easy nor clear cut. There is no right or wrong choice - only whatever choice you end up with. Choosing a career in massage isn't set in stone. Most people will have many careers throughout their lives and learn many things from each of them. You won't really know if a career in massage is for you unless you try it to find out what you like and don't like. Getting what we want is often a process of figuring out what we don't want. No matter what you choose, it will be right for you.

Monica Roseberry in the first edition of her book, *Marketing Massage*, traveled the country over a period of six months and asked massage therapists and massage schools just what it takes to be successful. What she found was that it has more to do with who they are than anything else.

As she points out in her book, a successful massage therapist has these four qualities:

1. A desire to serve
2. The commitment to succeed
3. A strong emphasis on professionalism
4. A commitment to excellent customer service

These four things depend on you and you alone. Your background, life situation, talents, or knowledge – do not really matter.

What makes the difference in whether or not you are successful in the massage profession is **YOU!**

Final thoughts - no matter how it works out you will at least be getting a massage every week and of course, getting your fill of folding laundry!

The best of luck to you. This is a great profession!

Chapter 12.
Career Resources

Online Articles

Alliance for Massage Therapy Association.
≤ http://www.afmte.org/online-training-center>.

American Massage Therapy Association.
< http://www.amtamassage.org>.

Bayer, Cary. "You Are in High Demand." Massage Today.
<http://www.massagetoday.com/mpacms/mt/article.php?id=13194>.

Benjamin, Ben E. "Envisioning the Future of Massage Therapy Education." 2006. Massage and Bodywork.
<http://www.massageandbodywork.com/Articles/AugSep2006/future.html>.

Blackburn, Jack. Articles on "Caretaking – A Hidden Addiction in Bodywork." 2005. Presencing.
< http://www.presencingsource.com/jacks-articles.html>.

Calvert, Robert Noah. "The Future of Massage in the New Millenium." The History of Massage. < http://books.google.com/books?id=Z-rVa50Vx94C&pg=PA227&source=gbs_toc_r&cad =3#v=onepage&q&f=false>.

Capellini, Steve. "Battleground Conditions in the Spa: Gearing up for Work in a Tough Industry." Massage & Bodywork. <http://www.massageandbodywork.com/Articles/OctNov2005/Battleground.html>.

Chute, Robert. "Man Power Male Therapists Talk About Discrimination." <http://www.massagetherapy.com/articles/index.php/article_id/1381/Man-Power> .

"Eliminating Caretaking Behavior." Livestrong.com. <http://www.livestrong.com/article/14672-eliminating-caretaker-behavior>.

Gill, Sandra. "Outcall Service and Safety: Preparation is the Key to Success." 2002. Massage & Bodywork. <http://www.massageandbodywork.com/Articles/JuneJuly2000/outcall.html>.

Goggins, Rick. "Ergonomics for MTs and Bodyworkers." 2007. Massage and Bodywork. <http://www.massageandbodywork.com/Articles/FebMar2007/ergonomicsformts.html>.

Grant, Alexis. "The 50 Best Careers of 2011." Dec. 2010. <u>U.S. News & World Report</u>. <http://money.usnews.com/money/careers/articles/2010/12/06/the-50-best-careers-of-2011>.

Grant, Keith Eric. "A Review of Issues in Massage Governance." April 2002. <http://www.ramblemuse.com/articles/masg_governance_rev.pdf>.

Hanlon, Phyllis. "The Challenges and Rewards of Hospice Massage." 2005. <u>Massage Magazine</u>. <http://www.massagemag.com/Magazine/2005/issue116/Hopice.php>.

<u>Hospital-Based Massage Network</u>. 2008. <http://www.naturaltouchmarketing.com/HBMN-hospital-massage/HBMNHome.php>.

"Instructors Resources." <u>Associated Bodywork and Massage Professionals</u>. <http://www.abmp.com/instructors/resources.php>.

Johnson, Ruthanne. "Cruise Industry Employment: The Pros & Cons." <u>Massage and Bodywork Magazine</u>. <http://www.massagetherapy.com/articles/index.php/article_id/585/Cruise-Industry-Employment>.

Keen, Lael Katherine. "The Ethics of Touch." <u>So-matics.</u> <http://www.somatics.de/>. Path: Articles; For Professionals; Mainly for Structural Integrators; The Ethics of Touch.

Korn, Cliff . "An Accreditation Quagmire." <u>Massage Today</u>.
<http://www.massagetoday.com/mpacms/mt/article.php?id=12063>.

Lowe, Whitney. "The Challenge Ahead for Massage Educators." <u>Massage & Bodywork</u>.
<http://www.massageandbodywork.com/Articles/AugSep2006/challenge.html>.

"Massage Therapy Fast Facts." Oct. 2010.
<u>Associated Bodywork and Massage Professionals</u>.
<http://www.massagetherapy.com/_content/images/Media/Factsheet1.pdf>.

<u>Massage Therapy Foundation</u>.
<http://www.massagetherapyfoundation.org>.

McKenzie, Walter. "Multiple Intelligences Inventory." 1999. <u>Walter McKenzie's One and Only Surfaquarium</u>.
<http://surfaquarium.com/MI/inventory.htm>.

Minton, Melinda. "Choosing the Spa That's Best for You." <u>Body and Spa</u>.
<http://www.massagemag.com/spa/treatment/choose.php>.

<u>My Massage Corner</u>.
< www.mymassagecorner.com>.

Nelson, Carl W. "Touch Points for Students." TheBodyWorker.com. <http://www.thebodyworker.com/touch_points_f rom_esalen.htm>.

Nelson, Carl W. "The Phenomenal Growth in Number of Massage Schools." TheBodyWorker.com. <http://www.thebodyworker.com/numberofmass ageschools.htm>.

Nicholson, Bernadette Della Bitta. "How to Choose a Massage Therapy School." Massage Magazine. <http://www.massagemag.com/Students/News/2 007/Choose-Massage-Therapy-School.php>.

"Occupational Employment Statistics." U.S. Bureau of Labor Statistics. <http://www.bls.gov/oes/current/oes319011.htm >.

"Occupational Outlook Handbook: Massage Therapists." U.S. Bureau of Labor Statistics. <http://www.bls.gov/oco/ocos295.htm>.

Osborn, Karric. "Gender in the Profession: Massage from Mars or Venus?" <http://www.massagetherapy.com/articles/index. php/article_id/1376/Gender-in-the-Profession> .

"Overcoming the Need to Fix." August 2010. Livestrong.com. <http://www.livestrong.com/article/14696- overcoming-the-need-to-fix>.

Patrick, Carrie. "Massage Profession Metrics."
<u>MassageTherapy.com</u>. ABMP.
<http://www.massagetherapy.com/media/metrics
.php>.

Patrick, Carrie. "Public Policy and Licensing."
<u>MassageTherapy.com</u>. ABMP.
<http://www.massagetherapy.com/media/policyo
verview.php> .

Polseno, Diane. "Enabling: The Dark Side of Being
Helpful." 2003. <u>American Massage Therapy Asso-
ciation</u>.
<http://www.amtamassage.org/uploads/cms/doc
uments/ethically_speaking.pdf>.

Remen, Rachel Naomi. "In the Service of Life."
1996. <u>Noetic Sciences Review</u>.
<http://www.rachelremen.com/service.html>.

Steiner Leisure. 2011.
<http://www.steinerleisure.com/main/Page.aspx?
PageID=5000>.

Stephens, Ralph. "Advice to Future Massage Therapists." June 2001. <u>Massage Today</u>.
<http://www.massagetoday.com/archives/2001/0
6/12.html>.

<u>Touch Research Institute</u>.
<http://www6.miami.edu/touch-research>.

Vanderbilt, Shirley. "Are We Doing Right By Students? Examining the Current State of Massage Education." <u>Massage and Bodywork Magazine</u>. 2002. <http://www.massagetherapy.com/articles/index. php/article_id/597/Are-We-Doing-Right-By-Students>.

Versagi, Charlotte. "Expert Advice." <u>Massage Magazine</u>. <http://www.massagemag.com/Magazine/2001/i ssue89/advice89.php>.

Books

Almaas, A.H. <u>Diamond Heart, Book One: Elements of the Real in Man</u>. Boston: Shambhala Publications, 2000.

Corey, Gerald, and Marianne Corey. <u>Becoming a Helper</u>. Belmont: Brooks Cole, 2006.

Dass, Ram. <u>How Can I Help?: Stories and Reflections on Service</u>. New York: Knopf, 1985.

Eker, T. Harv. <u>Secrets of the Millionaire Mind: Mastering the Inner Game of Wealth</u>. New York: HarperCollins, 2005.

Gerber, Michael E. <u>The E-Myth Revisited: Why Most Small Businesses Don't Work and What to Do About It</u>. New York: HarperCollins, 1995.

Hill, Napoleon. <u>Think and Grow Rich: Your Key to Financial Wealth and Power</u>. Mankato: Capstone, 2009.

McIntosh, Nina. <u>The Educated Heart: Professional Boundaries for Massage Therapists, Bodyworkers and Movement Teachers</u>. New York: Lippincott, 2005.

Orman , Suze. <u>Women and Money: Owning the Power to Control Your Destiny</u>. New York: Random House, 2007.

Paiva, Cidalia. <u>Keeping the Professional Promise</u>. Evansville: MT Publishing, 2004.

Remen, Rachel Naomi. <u>My Grandfather's Blessings: Stories of Strength, Refuge and Belonging</u>. New York: Penguin, 2001.

Roseberry, Monica. <u>Marketing Massage: From First Job to Dream Practice</u> . Albany: Milady, 2002.

Taylor, Kylea. <u>The Ethics of Caring: Honoring the Web of Life in Our Professional Healing Relationships</u>. Santa Cruz: Hanford Mead, 1995.
Valterra , Mikelann R. <u>Why Women Earn Less: How to Make What You're Really Worth</u>. Pompton Plains: Career Press, 2004

Massage School Questionnaire

1. What education requirements are there in my State _____, City_____ County_____ (Where you want to set up your practice or find a job?)

2. Is there an exam required for me to practice in this state, city, county? Is it the NCE, MBLex or a state exam? If no exam, are there plans in the works for setting up an exam? (If your state is not licensed, there may be regulations in each city.)

3. Are there any state, county or other regulations pertinent to setting up a massage business in my area? What are the requirements for setting up a business in my area? What business licenses will I need? Are there other things that are required? (Fingerprinting, background checks, etc.)

4. How many hours of education does your school offer?

5. What is the breakdown of the hours of courses? (How many hours of anatomy, physiology, pathology, massage theory, etc.)

6. What is required by the state to become licensed?

7. What classes are additional or optional? (Deep tissue massage, pregnancy massage, injury treatments, etc.)

8. What class schedules are available? AM? PM? Weekends?

    1. What happens if I miss a class?
    2. What happens if a teacher misses a class?

9. What is the focus of your program? Does it focus more on the technical aspects (medical massage, injury massage) or on energy/spiritual aspects (meditation, tai chi), or on psychological aspects, as in body/mind therapies?

10. How much does the program cost?

11. How much will the supplies cost including books, massage tables, accessories and any other fees?

12. When does the money have to be paid?

13. What scholarships or grants are available?

14. What financial aid can I get?

15. What payment plans are available?

16. How do I know your school will provide me with what I need to become a successful massage therapist?

17. What is the pass/fail rate of your students from last year? From 5 years ago? From 10 years ago?

18. How many students were in each class and how many graduated from your school? (This is an important because some schools will skew the data and by saying they have a really high percentage of students who pass the licensing exam when in fact they might have had many students who did not pass their school program. They take the students who have failed their school program out of the statistics.)

19. What is the success rate (own business, massage job) of your students from last year? From 5 years ago? From 10 years ago?

20. How many graduates have a full time practice?

21. How many graduates have a part time practice?

22. How many are not practicing at all?

23. Who are your teachers? Do they have credentials to teach?

24. What experience do they have in teaching?

25. What experience do they have in practicing massage?

26. Do they have or have they had full time practices in massage? Are they former graduates of the school? How many?

27. Are there certified counselors or mental health professionals available to you free of charge or for a small fee to talk to during the course of the program?

28. What are jobs in massage in this area like? How much can I really make?

29. What will my practice be like? How long will it take me to set it up and be able to make a living from it alone?

30. Can I bill insurance companies for massage? If yes, will I be able to become a provider for insurance companies? (In Washington State you can become a contracted provider but currently most of the lists are closed to new participants. They might forget to tell you that.) What requirements do insurance companies have for massage therapists? (This is a very important question is you want to become a provider.)

31. What range of jobs can I get in massage in this area? What pay and benefits can I expect?

32. What will be involved in setting up a business in this area? (License, registrations etc.) Does the school have resources that will help me build my business?

33. Is massage widely accepted by the public here?

34. What business classes and support will I get in school?

35. What kind of support will I have for building my practice or finding a job?

    1. Is there a job placement service?

    2. What is the success of this service?

    3. How are jobs listed?

    4. How often are they updated?

36. Is there a mentoring or apprenticeship program to assist me while I start my practice? Is there a supervision program during the course of school and after graduation?

37. How long will it take for me to find a job?

Career Resources

About the Author

Julie Onofrio, LMP is a self employed massage therapist in Seattle, WA since 1987 when she attended massage school. She is also the creator of many web-sites for the massage profession to help them through the many stages of becoming a massage therapist. If you still have questions about a career in massage, you can follow her at :

http://www.facebook.com/CareersInMassage

www.facebook.com/MassagePracticeBuilder

www.massage-career-guides.com

www.thebodyworker.com

Proof

Made in the USA
Charleston, SC
10 October 2011